The Stuff of a Life
Collected Essays

by
Paula Dunning

Embajadoras Press

Copyright 2022 © Paula Dunning

No part of this book may be reproduced or transmitted in any form or by any means, except for brief passages quoted by a reviewer, without written permission from the publisher—or, in the case of photocopying, a license from Access ©: the Canadian Copyright Licensing Agency

Cataloging data available from Library and Archives Canada
ISBN 978-1-988394-27-5 (paperback)
ISBN 978-1-988394-24-4 (ebook)

Published by Embajadoras Press
www.embajadoraspress.com

For my grandchildren:

Gavin, Aidan, Blake, Delaney,
Quentin, Stella, and Nina

May your lives be filled with the stuff of fine memories.

Acknowledgements

This collection has been a long time in the making and has benefitted from the input of many people along the way. Most particularly, I want to thank the members of my writing groups, fellow writers who share their comments and suggestions generously and honestly. Without them, I would not have the courage to publish. As the collection approached its final form, it benefitted from close reading by a number of arms-length volunteers, who offered a variety of perspectives and helped me look at the work with fresh eyes. My thanks to them for their careful attention to both the spirit and the letter of these essays.

And finally, I lovingly acknowledge and sorely miss the support that was always close at hand for whatever I set out to do. Until the final weeks of his life, Jack was encouraging me to move ahead with this project. And so, Jack, here it is.

• • •

A number of these essays have appeared in full or in part on my blog at *www.echoriver.ca*

A Note About Veracity

We are in an historical moment of widespread confusion about what is true, what is false, and where honest uncertainty fits into the puzzle of reality. It's a confusion that's familiar territory for a memoirist.

There are those who insist that memoir adhere precisely to verifiable facts. Others claim the right to embellish at will—or, as my mother-in-law used to say, "If a story is worth telling, it's worth making interesting." Given a life that stretches back to the 1940s, and both the limitations and the vagaries of memory, I find the former approach stifling and the latter tempting, as any storyteller would. However, I have resisted the urge to wander far off the path of my honest recollection of major life events and situations. I have allowed myself the freedom to embellish within the confines of "what must have been" so long as I am confident that I am not misrepresenting the spirit of the memories themselves or the integrity of the characters who appear in these pages. As for the characters themselves, I have changed the names of people from my past since most of them are no longer part of my life and there is no way for me to request their permission to appear on these pages.

I hope these essays, based on my memories and reflections, speak truths that extend beyond the details and circumstances of a single life.

Table of Contents

I	The Stuff of a Life	1
II	Not That it Matters	7
III	In Search of Grammy Smith	16
IV	Growing Up Quaker	29
V	My Father's World	46
VI	Thank You for the Pies	57
VII	The Unspeakable	70
VIII	Universal Divide	80
IX	Waiting for Armageddon	88
X	*In Loco Parentis*	95
XI	On Becoming Canadian	102
XII	Homemaking Squared	109
XIII	What Am I Bid for this Fine Piano?	117
XIV	Butter With That?	122
XV	Putting Up Signs and Hoping for the Best	129
XVI	The Boy from Belarus	138
XVII	It's Sunday. It's Mexico	149
XVIII	A Numbers Game	159
XIX	Seasonal Disorder	167
XX	Flowing On	174
	Afterward	178

I THE STUFF OF A LIFE

I wondered how people could live with things set in place, fixed, their places determined by the power of the recollection they contained, the memories they held. It was what made a home, I believed; the things we keep, the sum of us.

Richard Wagamese, Indian Horse

Dressed in a plaid, button-up shirt tucked into ironed blue jeans, with a string tie at his neck, Charlie began chanting at eleven sharp and didn't stop until the last item was sold late in the afternoon.

"And what-am-I-bid-for-this-fine-wheelbarrow, do-I-hear-thirty dollars? Thirty dollars?" Someone in the crowd called out a bid. "Ten dollars, I-hear-ten-dollars, just ten. Do I hear fifteen? Just-fifteen-dollars-for-this-wheelbarrow. Get-your-potatoes-to-the-cellar-in-record-time. I have ten." Then he spun to his left where someone had shouted out a number. "Twelve-fifty. I have twelve-fifty. Do I hear fifteen?" Patiently he milked the crowd until he was down to just two bidders. He looked first at one: "I have twenty dollars, just twenty dollars for this fine wheelbarrow. Will you bid twenty-five? Twenty-five?" The bidder hesitated, then nodded slowly. "Twenty-five. Now thirty," he said, fixing his gaze on the other bidder. "Do I hear thirty? I have twenty-five, do I hear thirty?" No one moved. In case anyone had missed it, he said it again: "Twenty-five dollars is bid for this wheelbarrow. Do I hear thirty?" He continued staring at the first bidder, who stood stolidly in place, slowly shaking his head. He'd reached his limit.

"Going once. Going twice. SOLD for twenty-five dollars." The successful bidder held up an index card with his bidder number printed in bold magic marker for Charlie's helper to record.

Charlie took a sip of water, pulled a handkerchief from his pocket to wipe his brow, and started again. "This here's a fine pig trough. Your little porkers'll thank you for this first-class dinner plate. Do I hear fifteen?"

It wasn't just wheelbarrows and pig troughs. I brought home stoneware crocks, table linens, rocking chairs, and stemware from these summer Saturday auctions in rural northern Ontario.

Local church women in polyester pants and colourful blouses sold ham-and-cheese or egg salad sandwiches, brownies, butter tarts, coffee and lemonade from long tables—planks on top of sawhorses, covered with flowered oilcloth. Small children played tag, darting among the bidders, or stood quietly by their parents, cowed by the confusion. Groups of friends sat on the grass and visited, waiting for their choice of items to come on the block.

Despite the carnival atmosphere, I felt an underlying melancholy at these auctions. There'd been a death, or a couple had grown too old to farm. How would it feel, I wondered—I still wonder—to spread out the acquisitions of my lifetime and see what people thought they were worth? I'm sure they'd never get it right. How could they, without knowing that the brass candlesticks came from my parents' trip to Russia and the tiny child's tea set with the taped-together sugar bowl had belonged to my grandmother? When I took home a framed photograph or a box of miscellaneous stemware, I knew I was claiming a small part of someone else's story, a story I would never know.

Auctions had been an occasional weekend destination for my family when I was a child. My dad enjoyed poking through boxes of miscellany, finding useful bits of hardware and treasures that reminded him of his own childhood. And books. Dog-eared, mildewed, but sometimes precious old books. The table and buffet that graced our dining room came from an auction, as did the revolving bookshelf that now sits in my own living room.

Hunting for treasures was a passion I carried into my own adulthood. Early in our marriage, Jack and I spent weekends roaming through antique shops and flea markets in rural southern Ontario. Soon after we began our "back to the land" adventure in northern Ontario, in 1972, we discovered farm auctions. Buckets of nuts, bolts, and electrical connections still reside in our basement nearly fifty years later. Decades after the original adventure petered out, there is no longer any conceivable use for a butter churn or an egg scale—except for the memories they conjure.

Now, of course, disposing of possessions has become a favourite pastime of the privileged. The Marie Kondo phenomenon has us all questioning whether the things surrounding us are "sparking joy".

I recently read that the average North American home contains an incredible 30,000 items. Staring at the collection of utensils in my kitchen drawers, the books on my shelves, the chaos in my sewing drawer, maybe it's not so incredible. How, I wonder, do you count the items? Every individual spoon? How about pieces of paper? Toothpicks? Spools of thread? Or the little tokens in the Monopoly game? Maybe it's closer to 300,000.

Everyone I know is sorting through stuff—that's "Stuff" with a sneer and a capital S—disposing of the unnecessary before the kids are left with the mess. I know people who've moved way beyond de-cluttering, have divested themselves of everything but the essentials, putting minimalism to the test. The experience, they say, has been liberating, soul-enhancing, their new lives light and free. God knows, my soul could use enhancing. I start with the bookshelves.

And there's that book of children's poems—the one with the blue cover that was a gift to my father from an old friend and has greetings penned inside the front cover. "To Warren, with thanks. Vincent, 1937." Eighty years ago, someone gave my dad this book as a gift. Thanks for what? Who was Vincent? And what dog chewed its cover? I don't know, and there's no one left who does. I open it and remember Dad reading my favourite poem aloud, the one about the glass boy. The book goes back on the shelf.

Three quilts are folded up in a wicker chest in the corner of the guest room. Two were made by one great-grandmother, the third by another. I didn't know either woman. All three quilts are carefully crafted but largely disintegrated; I have no use for them. I've had them on a pile to go more than once. But as a sometimes-quilter myself, they remind me of these women's existence, of their capable hands, and of their distant connection to me. I'm afraid they'll still be here when I'm gone.

And what about the lace tablecloth my grandmother made, tiny round circles the colour of oatmeal? My mom used it for special family dinners. It's stained so badly no one will ever use it again. I really should dispose of it. But when I unfold it, I see through the stain to Grammy Smith in her chair, her hands pulling delicate threads into intricate loops, her fingers growing stiff and the threads growing heavier as she grew older and gradually lost her sight. When I place the tablecloth beside the heavy, black-and-yellow crocheted afghan she made in her nineties, I have a record of her aging as clear as any photograph.

I never knew my paternal grandfather. I only know him from the stories my father told and wrote, stories of a small-town grocer in eastern Pennsylvania who outsmarted the new chain store across the street and invented things in his spare time. Things like a wagon brake that he patented just as horse-drawn wagons left the landscape, a rat trap that drowned rats in vats of water, and a wind-up flying machine that never flew. I have a model of the wagon brake in a small, hand-made wooden box with a metal clasp and varnish peeling off the top. It's the sample he sent to the patent office. I haven't opened it in years. It wouldn't bring ten dollars on the auction block. Nobody would know what it was.

He also made tin cookie cutters for his wife, my Grammy Smith, which I keep in the same little cardboard box my mother kept them in, wrapped in an old yellow paper napkin. First a Santa, elaborately detailed with a mittened hand, a cuffed boot, a tasselled hat, and a fur-trimmed jacket. Then a bird with a long beak and a delicate, gracefully arched, two-pronged tail. A simple wreath. And finally, a Christmas tree with branches spreading like curved fingers. If you're going to use these cookie cutters, you have to know that the best cookie recipe to use is the one for Grammy Smith's molasses cookies. The dough must be stiff and well-chilled; otherwise, the tassel on Santa's hat sticks in the cutter, the bird's tail separates from the bird when you move it to the cookie sheet, and the top of the tree breaks away from its trunk.

Would it enhance my soul to be rid of this stuff? Or does it nourish my soul to keep it? Is it joy I'm feeling, or nostalgia? And is one more valuable than the other? I wander through the house, stopping when I hear voices speaking to me from corners, cupboards, and drawers.

I pause in a corner of the living room at the revolving oak bookcase. It began its sojourn with our family at an auction, where Dad bought it more than sixty years ago. It's been in my own home for almost half that time, but it still speaks in Dad's voice, holds books he wrote, and conjures up memories of his life—a life that is no more real or important to me because I have his bookcase, but which has a permanent presence in my living room.

From somewhere on my dresser top, among pieces of jewellery I rarely wear, the voice of my grandmother—not the cookie-cutter one—calls out to me, reminding me that I have the first diamond ring my pappy gave her in the 1920s—three diamonds so small they are barely visible. He replaced it with a larger one at some point in their marriage, and as the oldest granddaughter, I was the recipient of the original. It doesn't fit me anymore. It's not my style. But I remember her giving it to me, sitting at her dining room table, telling me about her young and enduring love for Pappy.

George Eliot said, "Our dead are never dead to us until we have forgotten them." Maybe I will give the ring to my granddaughter, and bring her great-great grandmother back to life for a moment.

There are many reasons to examine our relationship with stuff, the way we allow it to define us, measure us, entrap us. I am not an apologist for acquiring or hoarding goods. On the contrary, it's clear that our acquisitiveness is threatening our very existence. Of course, I have more stuff than I need or, indeed, want. I, too, am sorting and tossing. But when things trigger memories and stories, I pause and remember. Often—maybe too often—I put them back on the shelf. Someday, I know, they will end up on an auction block or in a garage sale, their voices silenced. But in the meantime, what are we but the memories we hold and the stories we tell? And who am I to decide, in advance, what will trigger those memories for my children?

II NOT THAT IT MATTERS

A woman I barely know enters the dining room of my mom's retirement community where she and I are having an early supper. Mom looks up briefly, then shakes her head.

"Can you imagine wearing a plaid blouse with that striped skirt?"

She looks at her empty salad plate, embarrassed, and chastises herself for the unkind comment.

"Not that it matters."

But it does. It always has.

Mom studied to be a secretary and married her high school English teacher at eighteen. He was an "older man" of thirty-one. She was a mother at twenty. He was a college professor at thirty-three. She was Eliza Doolittle to his Henry Higgins.

The rain in Spain falls mainly on the plain.

The embryonic cells that were to be my mother were already madly multiplying by the time my sixteen-year-old Grammy married my not-much-older Pappy at the point of the proverbial shotgun. It was 1924 in the small, eastern Pennsylvania town of Bangor. The teen parents settled in with the bride's mother, my Great-Grammy Spangenberg, who ruled the roost with an iron, Methodist hand and cared for one, then two baby girls. The second was born less than a year after the first, prematurely; "small enough to fit in a mason jar" my grammy said, forever etching the image of a home-canned infant in the family's collective consciousness.

Neither Pappy nor Grammy graduated from high school. He worked in the rail yards and on a wrecking crew, and taught himself to repair radios and televisions as a sideline. She moved from one textile mill to another, sewing the sleeves on blouses or the ears on toy bunnies. The only reading material in their home was a Bible, the local newspaper, the TV Guide, and Pappy's repair manuals. Sometimes when Grammy read us stories, she stumbled over words in the Golden Books.

Not that it matters.

Until your husband is a university professor and you're thrust into the world of PhDs and their 1950s wives, who are the grown daughters of foreign diplomats, or bankers, or school principals. Graduates of Home Economics programs at the finest land-grant colleges, or liberal arts majors from Radcliffe, who don't know what a wrecking crew is and who never stop to wonder how the sleeves became attached to their blouses.

Until the conversation begins over cocktails, and you're not sure what you're supposed to do with the olive on a toothpick, and the liquid between you and the olive is caustic. Then, the woman on your left says, "Where did you go to school?"

And you know it shouldn't matter. Really. It shouldn't.

So you blush, and look down, and are so glad that your clothes, at least, are just right. You have to reply. "Well, actually, I was just a secretary."

Everybody nods and takes a sip from their funnel-shaped glass, and you try to see what they're doing with the olive so you can do the same thing. And hopefully, get to eat the olive.

"No ordinary secretary," says Dad with a twinkle, whenever the subject arises. "Smart as a whip." Which he is, of course, too kind to say in the presence of an ordinary secretary. "She could have done anything, but she married me."

You smile at him sweetly in those moments, but you're pretty sure you'd have been a secretary. An ordinary one.

You stir your drink and hope no one notices you checking your watch.

The woman in the red dress has a teenaged daughter who made the cheerleading team, and the one with the navy-blue high heels thinks her two-year-old son is coming down with chicken pox. You wonder if they're really all smarter than you, because you, too, can talk about your kids. That doesn't take a college degree.

Then the older woman—the one with the henna-red hair—carefully extracts the toothpick from the glass and plops the olive into her mouth, chewing slowly as though the morsel were a fine chocolate.

The library board is looking for volunteers, she says.

Is she looking at you? You look at your olive. Is it ready to be harvested? Is your toothpick far enough above the liquid to allow for a drip-free capture? You take another sip to be sure, careful not to wince.

You look across the room and see your professor-husband talking to a stout woman with cropped grey hair whose orange blouse is coming un-tucked from her too-tight lavender skirt. You stifle a smug smile and look down again at your smart grey suit with the black blouse and the pearls. Real pearls, they were your grandmother's.

Not that it matters, you say to yourself, carefully extracting the olive from the glass and sliding it off the toothpick with your front teeth.

Of course, it might not have been like that. You were a smart cookie, Mom—as Dad used to say before such language was considered demeaning. You probably figured out the olive on your own. And you never pretended to like gin. I am taking liberties with your younger self in my attempt to understand you, long past the time when I could ask. To understand the insecurities that continued to leak through the cracks in your competence. To understand why it mattered to you, and why it so often matters to me.

•••

My mom grew up in the 1920s and 1930s in a household dominated by her grandmother, that stern Methodist who did much of the child-rearing and homemaking while the naughty adolescent parents earned money and grew up. Even if they grew up slowly, they must have eventually chafed under her autocratic rule. She forbade drinking, card playing or any overt signs of frivolity. Until she died in 1950, they continued to live under her roof, and she continued to collect their pay cheques for household expenses, doling out spending money to the by-then middle-aged parents.

I remember Great-Grammy Spangenberg as an old woman—ancient in my small child's eyes—sitting in an armchair in the living room of the family home. In that living room, one of the earliest televisions mesmerized me with its rounded screen and the magic of Howdy Doody. Beside the television was a small desk with a phone—the very old kind without a dial. I was allowed to pick it up and talk to the operator, who was, miraculously, my Aunt Evelyn (she of the mason jar). Aunt Evelyn was the prettiest woman I knew, and I intended to become a telephone operator just like her.

In order to get to the television and the telephone, I had to walk past Grammy Spangenberg's chair. The old woman frightened me. She spoke in a loud voice and had warts growing on her face.

"Don't you step on that register now, Paula!" she shouted as I stepped off the bottom step onto the living room floor, skirting the iron grate that sent heat up from the coal furnace in the basement. Of course, she was warning me that the register was hot, a kindness; I'm sorry my memory is distorted by childhood fear. On a softer note, I also remember being taken into her upstairs bedroom when she was very ill, and sitting on the edge of her bed.

I stared at her sagging, deeply etched face, humourless but no longer threatening. She was partially upright, leaning against a propped pillow.

"Are you going to die?" I'd been listening to the grownups.

She reached her gnarled hand toward me and touched my face.

"Yes, Paula" she said. Matter of fact. "I'm going to die soon. Everyone dies."

If I should die before I wake, I pray the Lord my soul to take...

I don't remember being told she would be with God in heaven, but without a doubt she was confident of her destination.

Great-Grammy Spangenberg may have seen her granddaughters—my mom, Mae, and her sister, Evelyn—as a way of ensuring her status with the almighty since she never fully succeeded in domesticating her own unruly daughter, though she must have exhausted herself trying.

"She was the solid, steady one in our home," my mom said years later of her grandmother. "She was very strict, and we fought against all her rules. But she was always there for us. We knew she loved us."

My own grammy must have mourned the passing of her mother in 1950. But that passing liberated her and Pappy from the old lady's control. They sold the house she'd left to them and built a brand new bungalow on a country road beside a corn field, finally a home of their own. By then, in their early fifties, they had several grandchildren. As the oldest, at the age of six or seven, I was invited to help with the construction project. I hammered a nail in what would become the corner of their kitchen, a contribution to their home that none of us ever forgot.

"That's Paula's nail!" Pappy said, over and over, until I was old enough to roll my eyes in disinterest. Right under the kitchen table, beside the door to the hall, my nail, hidden by the white-and-beige linoleum.

Freed from the heavy hand of her mother, Grammy celebrated her mid-life emancipation by dying her thin, greying hair red, drinking sweet red wine, learning to drive, playing cards and bingo for money, and wearing halter tops over her ample and by then sagging bosom. She still attended church at Christmas and Easter, said grace before dishing out the pork chops and canned peas, and made passing reference to the Lord. But she put her own twist on the Lord's intentions.

"If God didn't want me to wear a halter top, he wouldn't have made such a sunny day," she explained to the fundamentalist neighbours next door. They shook their heads at her theological constructivism and drove off to their prayer meeting, where—I'm quite sure—they prayed for Grammy's soul.

It may have been too late. I'm not sure there was room in their Baptist heaven for a grandmother who offered her sixteen-year-old granddaughter a high-ball, gambled weekly, sang along and wiggled her hips to Elvis on the radio, and thought so little of her domestic responsibilities that she sent out the laundry on her factory-line earnings, and then—for want of a better use—kept potato chips in the clothes dryer. Whose favourite weekend activity was to shop at the five-and-dime and eat minute-steak sandwiches with onions at the lunch counter. Lots of onions, because Pappy hated onions, so she never had them at home. Who never turned her television off, and despite her general aversion to all things domestic had a kitchen overflowing with gadgets sold by those "call now, don't wait" television advertisers.

Who said to me, when I was about to marry, that she'd been very lucky to marry Pappy, whom she adored, because "it might have been someone else." Perhaps I read more into that than she intended, but in any case she got it right because both of her children and most of her grandchildren look like Pappy. Including me. For the next three generations, every new baby was greeted with Grammy's blessing and the assurance that the newest family member "looks just like Pappy." We are all quietly grateful that her own sharp features, with a long nose and pointed chin, resided on a recessive gene.

When Pappy died, Grammy missed him terribly and slipped into a long depression. But she never lost her raunchy sense of humour. Her last words, according to family myth, were, "With all these doctors poking at my tummy, I might get me another man yet."

Whatever heaven opened its doors to her, that's where I want to go.

• • •

"You made your pappy cry," Grammy said to me sternly as we carried our purchases into the house. They were visiting us for a few days. I'd never seen her angry like this before. Her already-thin lips were stretched even thinner.

I didn't have to ask why. I knew. I wiped tears off my own face, mumbled, "Sorry," and made a bee-line to my bedroom where I lay on my bed and sobbed in shame.

Lunch with Grammy and Pappy in town had turned into a battle of wills. They wanted to eat at the lunch counter at Woolworths. I wanted to go to the Corner Room—where the booths were filled with university students smoking and having deep conversations. Where my high school friends and I hung out after school, imagining ourselves indistinguishable from the university crowd.

It was my kind of place. I wanted them to see.

I don't remember where we finally ate. Perhaps we didn't in the end. I just remember the heavy weight that settled in my chest when Pappy said, "I guess we're not good enough to eat with the likes of you anymore."

In retrospect, and if my memory isn't doing him an injustice, I'm not sure who was the more adolescent in that stand-off. But the weight of guilt surely falls on me, because of course, in some sense, that's exactly what I was implying. That I could introduce them to a higher-class experience than the lunch counter at Woolworths. That I could read them the Latin inscription on the Corner Room wall. *Haec olim meminisse juvabit*: Perhaps someday it will be a joy to remember this.

"Virgil? You never heard of him?"

Not that it matters.

All they really wanted was lunch.

• • •

I return to the imagined cocktail party where my mother may or may not have known what to do with the olive. I move her forward a decade and a half, and she is now comfortable as a faculty wife—never quite confident that she "fits in", but confident enough to enjoy where her life has taken her. With her professor-husband, she attends concerts and plays, begins to explore ideas and to take tentative steps into the academic world.

And I imagine her parents—those naughty teenagers—now in their late middle age, spending several days a year on the periphery of her new life. They are impressed by our family, somewhat in awe of their son-in-law, proud of their daughter. But is her life something of a mystery to them? No doubt. Does she sometimes flaunt her new-found comfort with the arts, ideas, and academia? She may. These things matter to her now.

And her daughter? Her daughter, at sixteen, has learned—probably from her mother—that "fitting in" matters. She has also learned that the trappings of sophistication can send powerful messages. What she hasn't learned yet is that how those messages are sent, and to whom, determines whether they impress or injure.

I made my pappy cry. Across the generations, I'm sorry.

III IN SEARCH OF GRAMMY SMITH

We often had schnitzen parties. Then we did square dancing, played Post Office and Pussy in the Corner...We would stand around the piano and sing...Those were the perfect days.
                                From "Recollections of Grammy Smith"

It's a Sunday afternoon in 1955, and we are in the Packard station wagon, on our way to Sunbury. As we start to drive over the Allegheny Mountains, Dad sings, "Over the mountains and through the woods, to Grandmother's house we go."

We are going to Grammy Smith's house, two hours away. She lives with my Aunt Sarah and Uncle Ray. Aunt Sarah is Dad's sister, and we have to visit them for Sunday dinner about once a month.

In the car on the way, Mom reads the *New York Times News of the Week in Review* out loud to Dad while Rodney and I sit in the back seat. He's very squirmy, and I wish he'd just sit still. I'm staring out the window, imagining that I live on one of the farms we drive by. I'd love to live on a farm. I'd put my hair in pigtails so it wouldn't get in the way when I did my chores. Like feeding chickens and milking a cow. But wait...that little cabin we just passed going up the mountain is very cute too. It might be fun to live there. I could feed the wild animals and walk on paths through the forest as quiet as an Indian. I already have moccasins.

Grammy Smith is very old. Almost eighty. She's small and thin, and she wears her hair in tight little braids pinned in a circle at the back of her neck. She's always wearing an apron over her Sunday dress when we get there.

"*Wie geht's*, Warren," she says to Dad, and they say a few words in Pennsylvania Dutch before going back to English.

Then everybody hugs everybody else. Grammy Smith's hug is kind of stiff, more like a pat on the back; Aunt Sarah's is very big so you fall into her soft body that smells sweet, like bath powder. I'd really rather not have to hug Uncle Ray; he smells like tobacco and he hugs too hard. He wears black suits, smokes cigars, and sells insurance. He carries hard candies in his pockets which he gives to us kids to make us like him. It doesn't work very well.

Aunt Sarah works at a home for blind people, so she knows some braille which is the only interesting thing about her that I can see. She was born with some kind of spine problem, so she's a bit lopsided. Mom says that's why she never had any kids, so we don't have any cousins there. I think she likes to pretend I'm her kid, but I don't think I'd want her for a mom.

Visiting this Grammy isn't anything like visiting the young Grammy and Pappy. There's no television, for one thing. And everything is kind of dark and gloomy. The living room is covered in wallpaper with huge dark jungly vines, and the drapes are never open.

Grammy brings out the only toys in the house: a doll and a little orange kitchen cupboard with tiny cups and saucers for me, some cars and trucks for Rod. I don't think she realizes that I'm almost ten now and a little old to play dolls. So, I sit in the big chair in the corner with the biography of Amelia Earhart that I've brought along to read. I just finished Clara Barton. I'm going to read about all the famous people in the orange biography books.

The ottoman in front of the chair is piled with old newspapers, Perry Mason mysteries for Uncle Ray and copies of a magazine, *The Lutheran Woman*, for Grammy and Aunt Sarah. Even in the bathroom there are copies of *The Lutheran Woman*. Grammy and Aunt Sarah are very Lutheran women. Aunt Sarah doesn't understand why Dad's a Quaker now. She thinks everyone should be a Lutheran. I don't know what Grammy thinks. She mostly talks to Dad.

When Grammy stands in the archway between the living room and the dining room and takes off her apron, that means it's time to eat. Behind her, the oak table is opened to its largest size and set with the good dishes—white, with little blue windmills and ships. I take my seat, and while Grammy is saying grace I check out the food: some kind of meat with gravy, boiled potatoes, corn, cooked cabbage, pickles, and bread. The usual.

"…which we are about to receive. Amen."

The grownups talk about people back in Bangor, their home town in eastern Pennsylvania—people I've never heard of—while I try to get extra pickles and avoid eating the boiled cabbage.

I notice a lull in the conversation and look up. I am all ears, but too late.

Aunt Sarah's lips are clenched tight and Mom is looking down at her plate. Grammy is staring at something out the window. Dad puts his hand on Mom's shoulder and looks at Aunt Sarah. "Sis," he says, "it was a long time ago. Maybe it's time to relax about it."

Aunt Sarah does a sort of harrumph thing, and everybody goes back to their food. But I can tell something has happened. I think I might make a good detective. Like Nancy Drew.

As children, we thought of it as "Grammy Smith's house", but when I cast my memory back to those endless Sunday dinners, it's Aunt Sarah's voice I hear while Grammy sits at the end of the table, listening but rarely speaking, eating her boiled potatoes dipped in a little dish of warm milk with melted butter. "Grammy Smith potatoes", we called them.

On the way home Mom complains to Dad that it's always the same meal and Dad says yes, it's the same meal he ate every

Sunday of his life, and then he ate the leftovers all week long. Sometimes it was chicken. Then he and Mom start talking about what they ate when they were little, and I tune them out to stare out the car window at the dimming light.

"We won't get home 'til after dark," I hear Mom say.

The mountains are fading into the twilight. Rodney is beside me, half asleep, his head leaning against the window. Away from me, thank goodness, and he's not squirming. I'm staring out at the passing lights, imagining that I live in a tiny trailer like the one we passed awhile back. It's full of special furniture, and everything fits into little spaces. There's a bed that turns into a sofa during the day and a sink that turns into a shower.

I hear Dad say, "I wish you hadn't mentioned Lucy."

I abandon the little trailer to listen. Nancy-Drew-like.

"You know Sarah," he says.

"It's a long time ago, and she was your grandmother. Sarah's too."

"That's not the point."

"Yes, yes. I know, and I'll try not to mention her again. It's just all so silly."

Quiet. I guess the conversation is over. Dad's grandmother? What was wrong with her?

I try to return to my tiny trailer, but it's not there anymore.

We began referring to her as "The Mysterious Lucy", mother of the grandfather I never knew, who had given birth to him in in the 1870s and raised him without benefit of a husband. The topic of conversation was forever verboten in the presence of Grammy Smith and Aunt Sarah, though my father spoke openly and admiringly of Lucy, whose lover had belatedly offered his hand in marriage and was sent packing. It is, as far as I know, the closest to scandal that side of the family ever came, although there was always a sense of unspoken secrets in that dreary house, something hidden beneath the antimacassars and copies of old newspapers and *The Lutheran Woman* that covered every surface.

As I grew older and more attuned to adult interactions, I realized that Aunt Sarah didn't like my mother. Was it because Mom's mother, that spunky young Grammy who wore halter tops on Sundays, had felt little shame for bringing a child into the world under only slightly more acceptable circumstances than Lucy's? Maybe. Did Grammy Smith feel the same way? I don't know. There is so much about her I don't know.

• • •

With few exceptions, our impressions of people are trapped in the bubble of time when our lives intersect. When I was born, my mother's mother was in the prime of her life, not yet forty. As I moved through childhood and into the prime of my own life, I saw that grandmother moving, too. I remember when, in her mid-forties, she finally learned to drive—hitting a dog crossing the road on the way to her driving test, but passing it anyway. I remember her raunchy sense of humour and her fondness for popular music. She liked Elvis before I did. I remember her leg-rubs, the soothing, rhythmic movement of her fingers along my calves while we sat together and watched TV. I remember her struggle with depression and alcohol as she lurched through menopause when I was in my teens, and her grief and return to depression when Pappy, her much-loved husband, died. And I remember my own grief when she died in her early eighties. I had known her for half of her life.

My father's mother, on the other hand, was always old, my memories of her framed by the narrow lens of those Sunday dinners and annual Christmas visits, where the gifts were practical and the small Christmas tree faded into the background of the botanical wallpaper.

Throughout my childhood, a picture of her hung in my dad's study. Hair pulled back, rimless glasses, wide lace collar topping her dark dress, she sits straight and looks directly into the camera with a serious but gentle expression. She is holding her left hand limply in the grasp of her right, so that, as children, we puzzled about what it was she held.

"It's her other hand," Dad explained to me more than once. But I couldn't see it that way. It appeared to be some inanimate object she clutched. Apparently I wasn't alone. When I told my brother

Selden that the photo now hangs in my own study, he said "Oh that picture. The one where she's holding a pickle!"

On Dad's wall, she was an ancient woman; now, on mine, she is my contemporary and I find myself looking at her solemn, intelligent face—not so old, really—searching for signs of our shared genes.

It's clear that she is holding her hands sedately in front of her.

Those hands, in my memory, are busy with a crochet hook or stirring gravy at the kitchen stove. I couldn't have imagined my sedate Grammy Smith in her housedress and sturdy black lace-up shoes as a lively girl playing post office, or even as a younger woman with an active family life. But then, what child's imagination can peel the years off an aging grandparent?

• • •

In December, 1975, the year I turned thirty, a small parcel appeared in our mailbox, a Christmas gift from my father. On the yellow, construction-paper cover of an eight-by-eight booklet, Dad had used his limited artistic ability to sketch a horse-and-buggy beside a couple leaning against a tree. Written across the top, in a script tidier than his own—probably Mom's—was the title: *Recollections of Grammy Smith*.

Inside, pages of Grammy's memories were interspersed with photos from her younger life and some occasional elaboration from Dad. During the war, he had asked his mother to write some of the stories she had shared with her children, but he didn't realize she had done so until, nearly a decade after her death, Aunt Sarah presented him with a box of odds and ends. "Among these things," writes Dad, "was a notebook for German which I had used my first year at college (1929-30)...Mom discovered that I had written only on every other page, leaving the reverse sides of the pages blank, and, always frugal, she used these pages to record her recollections." I use them to peel back those years, trying to enliven the bare facts with glimpses of the woman behind the apron.

> *I can remember when I went to school when but four years old...everybody talked Dutch [Pennsylvania Dutch], but our books were all English. We learned to read and write. I could read swell, but didn't understand anything I read so it was all Greek...the teachers were just as Dutch.*

Is this why, in my family, "You're talkin' dutch" meant "It's all Greek to me."?

One of the few memories I have of Grammy outside the house was a trip to a five-and-ten-cent store, where I bought a wallet. She tried to dissuade me. "When you buy the wallet, you won't have any money left to put in it," she warned. Apparently at five I was already confident of a steady source of income, a luxury I suspect she never took for granted.

> *We were pleased more with a penny than the young people now days with a dollar...I remember on Christmas we could buy Christmas candy with the pig bristles we combed out. We always butchered and saved the bristles for our candy. We used to get ten cents to go to the Nazareth fair once a year, and that was a treat. One year I sneaked thirty cents apiece for me and my sister Alice, then we bought each a plate of ice cream, that was the first ice cream we ever ate, and we were scared to death our brothers would see us eat it and tell the folks. Then we couldn't enjoy the ice cream.*

It seems the family supplemented its farm income with a flour mill, and when that burned down they struggled to make ends meet on their forty acres of land until the boys were old enough to learn a trade and they all moved to town.

> *I believe it was in 1888 on the first of April we moved to [town]. We come up with a load of furniture on a Friday, then the rest all come on Monday. Aunt Alice come on a load of hay. I bet the people thought we were gypsys. We were all so dutch, but there were people who could talk it at that time. We soon got acquainted, the girls come for the boys and don't wonder but that some boys also come for us girls...in a short time we were all singing in the choir and everybody got along swell.*

And here is my sedate Grammy at her coy best.

> *I was always full of fun when young, still like things lively. When I was young there were no movies or no nothing. If we wanted to go anywhere, we had to go with some one that had a horse and carriage...well, there was a fellow by the name of John Frey. He liked me*

a lot. He drove two horses and had a swell carriage. He asked me to go to the Nazareth fair. I accepted. I did want to go to the fair. We went in great style, he wore a high hat, and drove the two horses. We had a swell time. Of course, I didn't like the fellow. He wanted to make dates with me after that, but I wouldn't have him...Done the same trick to another fellow. Always wanted to go over the mountain where my grandparents lived and my mother came from. I went again, his name was Eugene Gower. He took me to his home, had a big dinner there, his parents seem to be so proud that he had Sally Drumheller's daughter for a girlfriend...but I never thought of having him for a boyfriend and only went with him to get over the mountain.

Here are the bare facts. Grammy Smith was one of seven surviving children growing up on a farm in Bushkill County, Pennsylvania in the 1870s and 1880s, where the language at home was Pennsylvania Dutch. She married young, had a daughter, and lost her first husband in her mid-twenties. During those years, she moved often and, it seems, lived a life of financial insecurity. When she later married my Grandpa Smith, son of the Mysterious Lucy, she seems to have settled into a comfortable life, wife of a small-town grocer, eventually mother of four.

She was widowed for a second time in 1937, at the age of sixty-four, but I don't know when and under what circumstances she sold the family home and moved in with Aunt Sarah and Uncle Ray—certainly before my earliest memories of her. Had her playful younger self already mellowed to the kind but solemn grandmother I remember? Or, was it always there behind the apron, invisible to a child who couldn't see past the aging body? As one who now lives in such a body, with young grandchildren of my own, I find this prospect troubling.

If Grammy did, indeed, "still like things lively", I imagine she found life in that house on Front Street stifling.

•••

It's another Sunday and another dinner. This time it's pork with sauerkraut. The potatoes are mashed. I'm waiting for Mom and Dad to tell Grammy Smith that we're going to have a new baby. It's not a secret anymore, but they haven't told her yet. They told my other Grammy, and she's very excited. But I heard Dad tell Mom that Grammy Smith won't be happy about it. I perked my ears up at that. Why wouldn't anyone be happy about a baby?

I don't think Mom and Dad know that when I put my ear against the radiator pipe that runs from my bedroom down to the kitchen, I can hear everything they say.

"You know Mom," Dad was saying. "She worries about everything. Especially about babies."

Mom giggled sort of funny and said, "I don't think she was crazy about making them either."

Then Dad whispered something and I didn't hear any more. I think they left the kitchen.

But now, we're here at her house, eating dinner, and still they haven't told her. Maybe I will. Maybe I should just say…Oh. Dad's talking now. Here it comes.

"Well Mom," and what? He's started talking Dutch to her. Then she smiles at Mom, so I guess she knows now. She seems happy enough. Mom says it's far enough along now, no need to worry.

It was true. Grammy Smith did worry about everything, as we learned during the very brief chapter of family life, "In Which We Saved Grammy Smith from the Flood."

The house in Sunbury was on Front Street, directly across from the dike that protected the city when the Susquehanna River flooded in the spring. All these decades later, I am questioning my memory, wondering if once again Google knows best. It seems nothing officially recorded as a flood took place in Sunbury during the years when these events must have occurred. So perhaps we didn't actually save Grammy Smith from anything. But I know this much: Aunt Sarah phoned to tell us that city officials were asking people on Front Street to leave their homes because they feared the river would rise above the dike.

"She and Ray are staying put, but she thinks it would be best if Mom came here for a while until the water recedes," said Dad after he hung up the phone. "I'll drive over to Sunbury after lunch and bring her back."

We spent the afternoon making up a bed in Dad's study and picking up small toys that might cause Grammy Smith to trip and fall. The "baby", who was now my three-year-old brother Selden, crawled around barking. He was in his "I'm a dog" phase.

When Grammy arrived with a small suitcase, Selden nipped at her ankles.

"Selden, stop now," said Mom, lifting him off the floor.

"Arf. I'm a dog."

"No, you're a boy and your Grammy wants a hug."

I thought Grammy wanted to get as far from him as possible.

"Arf."

During her several days with us, Grammy Smith worried about the house in Sunbury and the rising water. She worried about Aunt Sarah. She worried that Rodney didn't eat enough. She worried that she was in the way. She worried about Dad driving home from work and about me and Rodney walking home from school. But mostly, she worried about Selden.

"Mae, do you think he really thinks he's a dog?" she asked.

"No, Mom. He's just playing."

"He never stops, though. Do you think there's something a little bit wrong with him?"

"No, no. He wasn't a dog last week. This is new." Mom hesitated. "Last week he was a duck." She looked at Rodney and me, gave a little wink, and we all started to sing:

There's a little white duck, sitting in the water
A little white duck, doin' what he oughta...

Grammy Smith put down her crocheting and looked at Mom. You could see the worry just pouring out of her. I think maybe she was worried about all of us.

"This isn't right, Mae. None of my children did this. Is he ever just himself?"

The little dog came running on two feet into the living room, then dropped onto all fours. "Arf. I'm hungry. Arf."

After a few days, the water receded, Dad drove Grammy Smith home, and shortly thereafter Selden's dog phase came to an end. I don't remember what he was next.

• • •

During my late childhood and early adolescence, I often spent a week during the summer with Grammy Smith. In her eighties, she was still healthy and active. I stayed in a small, sparsely-furnished bedroom with a gabled window looking out on the street, the dike, and the river behind it. Its bare simplicity made me think of the convents I'd read about, and given the religious tone of the household it seemed only natural that my fantasy life would involve vows of silence and walking close to the walls. I'm not sure anyone noticed. I even paged through the Bible that was thoughtfully provided on my bedside table, though I preferred reading Uncle Ray's Perry Mason mysteries.

Aunt Sarah and Uncle Ray went to work every day, so I was with Grammy. We weeded the little vegetable garden in the back yard, picked and podded peas, and prepared supper. Sometimes we played gin rummy. Once she asked me to choose something from the china cabinet, a special piece that would eventually be mine. I was not interested in china, but she insisted so I chose a soup tureen. She meant it to be mine, I'm sure, but it never found its way to me.

It saddens me to think that I am one of the few people still living who remembers Grammy Smith, and I remember so little. Even if it's true that people don't really die as long as one person remembers them, her days are numbered. In my memory, she is eighty-five, still cooking and gardening, still braving the basement stairs to fetch a jar of pickles from the storeroom. Even at rest, her hands are busy with a crochet hook, crocheting lace tablecloths for everyone in the family, then woolen afghans as her eyesight begins to fail.

In her late eighties, she broke her hip and never regained her mobility. By her early nineties, she could no longer see well enough to crochet. She sat most of the day in her chair in the living room, worrying about the people on the television—or in the television, I should say, because she was convinced that they were going to emerge and do harm. The chance to know her better was gone.

Before Jack and I got married, we went to Sunbury so she could meet him, but she was too confused to understand. When the call came later that year, I didn't feel much grief. I was in my early twenties, just married, in grad school, self-absorbed. I didn't go home for the funeral. I didn't really mourn her until years later when I read my dad's little booklet, filled with her memories and photos from more than a century ago—and I was overcome with sorrow for all the stories and all the wisdom, for all the opportunities that are lost in the hubbub of life and the inevitability of death.

IV GROWING UP QUAKER

At the bottom of the pile of music books in my piano bench is a maroon, hard-covered volume with gold lettering on the front: *A Hymnal for Friends*. I remember when these replaced the thinner, dark green hymnals that sat on the Meetinghouse benches. I can feel the stiff brown cushions that tried to soften those hard benches, see the meeting room with windows—unadorned by drapes or blinds—lining both sides and a fireplace in front, feel the serenity of a community sitting in silence. I turn the pages until I find my favourite. "Dear Lord and Father of mankind, forgive our foolish ways...": The lyrics are too traditional to reflect my current beliefs, but they still resonate. "Speak through the earthquake, wind, and fire, O still, small voice of calm."

•••

It is 1952. I am in the second grade. I come home from school in my plaid dress with the white collar and a bow at the back, carrying my new pencil case — the kind with a ruler for a lid that slides back and forth and has a pencil sharpener on one end. I am proudly singing the latest playground tune.

> *Whistle while you work,*
> *Stevenson's a jerk,*
> *Eisenhower's got the power,*
> *Stevenson's a jerk.*

When the kitchen door slams behind me, Mom turns away from the stove, where she's making pudding for dessert. "Do you know who Stevenson is?" she asks. "Or Eisenhower?"

Of course I do. "They both want to be president but Stevenson is too stupid. Everybody says. So you shouldn't vote for him." My six-year-old self wasn't entirely wrong. It was the middle of Pennsylvania, and most people did say that.

At the supper table, over pork chops and apple sauce, Mom and Dad explain to me that Eisenhower is a Republican, and Republicans are sort of war-like. Peace-loving people, they say, will vote for Stevenson, who is a Democrat. And in any case, the song I was singing isn't very nice. They use words like "pacifist" and "co-existence", which I don't really understand.

At school the next day, I explain to my teacher that all the members of my church — which isn't really a church exactly but a Meetinghouse where people can believe whatever they want because God lives inside them — are Democrats. My teacher raises her eyebrows and wonders what sort of church that is.

I continue to hum the song, but I don't say the words out loud.

•••

At thirty-four, my dad was a seeker who'd had enough of sin and damnation. He was looking for a gentler god, and he found him in the State College Friends Meetinghouse, a simple, white clapboard building just across the street from the apartment building where he, Mom, and baby me lived for Dad's first year as a Theatre Arts Professor at Penn State. I do believe in coincidence, but for those who don't this would be a sliver of evidence for the invisible hand of fate.

For the first while after Dad discovered Quakers, Mom continued to send me to the Methodist Sunday School. She was already living outside her comfort zone, and perhaps this was a step too far. But by the time I was singing about Stevenson we had become a Quaker family. Quakerism, along with the academic environment of a university town, became a principal incubator of my childhood.

We called it First Day School instead of Sunday School, a throw-back to the days when the gentle people known at first derisively and then proudly as Quakers, substituted numbers for the days and months named after pagan deities; when they wore plain grey clothing, spoke in Biblical English, and considered music a dangerous invitation to a false piety. When they earned their epithet (they called themselves Friends of Jesus or Friends of Truth) by quaking, or trembling, before the Lord.

But by the mid-twentieth century, for these enlightened Quakers of central Pennsylvania, First Day was cheerfully followed by Monday and Tuesday; the lady who played the piano for First Day School songs wore a purple dress every week, often with a matching hat; and the assembled worshippers ended their silent meeting with three hymns — although one elderly member regularly felt called upon to remind them that they should not allow themselves to be carried away by words of excessive zeal.

I never saw anyone quake. Never.

• • •

We live in the village of Lemont, halfway up Nittany Mountain. Lemont has a gas station where you can buy soda, candy, and comic books, and two little grocery stores, Boles and Shueys. Boles has a green front, Shueys has a red front. People in town are very particular about where they shop. There are Boles people and Shueys people. We're Shueys people. I don't know why. Sometimes on the way home from school I stop at Shueys to buy a chocolate bar. Most chocolate bars cost five cents, but there's one, with a green wrapper, that's only three cents, so for a nickel I can buy one of those and two tootsie rolls.

Shueys is okay, but I wish we were Boles people, partly because you can charge things at Boles, but also because the other half of Boles store is a house with a big front porch and a special secret place in the basement that was used to hide slaves as part of the underground railroad. I like to pretend I'm a slave, especially when I have to iron all Dad's handkerchiefs. Usually, I am an escaped slave girl taken in by a kindly Quaker family that uses a lot of handkerchiefs. Sometimes I've been beaten by my owner or stolen from my mother before I escaped and was rescued by the Quakers from the basement next door to Boles. I tie my light brown hair back in a kerchief and wish my eyes and skin were brown.

Sometimes, when I don't feel like being a slave, I pretend I am Lucretia Mott. I read about her in one of the orange books of biographies for young people. I read a lot of those orange books — Ben Franklin, George Washington, William Penn, Clara Barton. I really like Lucretia because she was a Quaker and she fought against slavery because even slaves have the inner light.

Now I am sitting in the back seat of a car, singing a little song to myself. It's not our car. I'm with friends, coming back from swimming, or maybe a birthday party. I want the other people in the car to know that I am a peace-loving child of Quaker parents, which makes me just a bit better than they are. This is very un-Quakerly, but that doesn't occur to me. I am only eight, but I know that most people are really into bombs and stuff like that, but we're not. We're pacifists, which I now know means that we don't believe in war. So it's too bad that Eisenhower won, but at least there's no war.

I'm singing just loudly enough for everyone in the car to hear the lyrics and become better, more peaceful people as a result, but not so loudly that I'm showing off. I sense this is a delicate balance, but I'd really like someone to ask me how it feels to be a Quaker and to believe that there is a little piece of God in me. And in everybody else, too, of course. So I end up singing right out.

There's a light that is shining in the heart of man,
There's a light that's been shining since the world began,
There's a light that is shining in the Turk and the Jew,
There's a light that is shining, Friend, in me and in you.
Walk in the light, wherever you may be...

Nobody pays any attention.

• • •

Before I could read for myself, my parents bought a little book called *The Garden We Planted Together*, published by the brand new United Nations. It featured children from all over the world, dressed in their traditional garb, turning the soil, hoeing, planting, weeding, harvesting, and sharing the fruits of their cooperative labour. A little Dutch girl in her crisp apron and wooden shoes prepared the row for the Japanese girl in her kimono who followed behind planting the seeds and who was, in turn, followed by the Mexican boy in bare feet and a sombrero covering the seeds with soil, and the Eskimo in his mukluks with a watering can. The book was accompanied by a 78-rpm record of cheery children's songs about cooperation and brotherly love. This was the world as it should be. It wasn't yet. But if we all tried—if we planted this sunny garden together—we could create a better world.

I sang along with the rest of the First Day School children.
This world our home is big,
But not too big to be
A place where friendliness, dear God,
Makes us one family

In the summer of 1951, to help make the world one family, my parents took me and my little brother, Rodney, along to Mahwah, New Jersey—now, I believe, a classy New York suburb but then a town inhabited by the people referred to as Jackson Whites or "Mountain People", an isolated community living in poverty. Mom and Dad were going as directors of an American Friends Service Committee (AFSC) "work camp". Their summer project consisted of renovating the community church. There, at the age of six, I first encountered people not at all like myself—poor, hard-drinking, gospel-singing folks who became my family's community for the summer and used language that made my mom squirm.

The campers themselves were middle-class teenagers who were being exposed to the ideals of community service and the principles of tolerance. When they weren't working or being otherwise exposed to lofty ideals, the boys lay on the floor watching Jessie, the woman whose house we were living in, walk by. Apparently she wore no underpants. When Mom and Dad discovered this diversion, they asked the woman in question to cover up. Tolerance had its limits. I don't know whether they also asked the boys to get off the floor, and I don't know what the girls were doing while the boys amused themselves in this way.

I didn't like Jessie much because she thought my little brother was very, very cute—which I knew he wasn't—and paid no attention to me at all. And what kind of grownup has to be told to wear underpants?

• • •

Four years later, and we are driving south along the eastern seaboard in a pale green Fraser sedan. There are still just four of us. Rod is six and I am nine. We are sitting in the back seat. Frisky, our cocker spaniel is in the trunk with the door propped open, in a special crate Dad built for him. Dad also built a platform for the top of the car, which is piled with suitcases. Mom rolls down her window to let the warm southern air blow through her long brown hair and begins to sing.

I've been workin' on the railroad...

We are on our way to South Carolina, where Mom and Dad are going to be directing another AFSC work camp in a town called Frogmore on St. Helena Island. Rod and I laugh at the weird name.

"More frogs!"

"Frogs some more!"

Everybody who lives on the island is a Negro. Everybody. I guess that's why Grammy is all upset. I'm not supposed to know that, but I heard her talking to Aunt Evelyn when we visited them at their house last week.

"I just can't believe Mae and Warren are doing this," Grammy was saying. "They don't even know where they'll be living. And with people like that! And taking the kids!" She was shaking her head and it sounded like she was going to cry.

That's when Aunt Evelyn noticed me and shushed Grammy up. But it made me kind of wonder and a little bit worried.

I don't know any Negroes, but Mom and Dad say that they really are just like us inside, only a different colour on the outside. So that's okay.

(I note here some discomfort using the terminology of the 1950s, but the word Negro was, at that time, the respectful term to use when referring to African-Americans.)

We drive for two days, and when we finally get there we move into the downstairs of a very large old house with a big front porch. Upstairs in the bedrooms there will be twelve teenagers.

During the day the teenagers, who are all white, will be painting and repairing some buildings that used to be a school for Negro children. Mom and Dad will be in charge. Rod and I will be…well…we'll find all kinds of interesting things to do, Mom is sure of that.

It turns out to be true. I don't actually know what Rod does, but I make friends with a lady who is a school teacher. I didn't know! Negroes can be school teachers! She lives in a little house filled with books, lots of them for kids, and she lets me visit and borrow books whenever I want. I also make friends with an old man who walks with a cane and wears a straw hat over his black hair. He has a big garden filled with flowers and bushes that are all labelled. I'm a very good reader, but I can't read his labels. He says it's because they're in Latin, which nobody speaks anymore — but I guess maybe he does. There are paths that go in among the plants with little benches, and I'm allowed to go there whenever I want to and sit on the benches with my borrowed books.

My best friend on St. Helena Island, Joseph, is ten. Joseph's mom is the cook for all the teenagers and for us, too. We all eat in a building that's a kitchen and a big room filled with picnic tables, with some rooms in the back where she and Joseph live.

His mom is very, very good at finding ways to eat hot dogs because someone made a mistake and ordered twelve cases of hotdogs instead of twelve packages. We have hot dogs and eggs for breakfast, hot dogs for lunch, and hot dogs in spaghetti sauce for supper, until all the hot dogs are gone. Then, we have to eat shrimp that she buys from a boat.

Joseph and his mom are Negros too. I know I'm not supposed to care. And I don't care, really, but I am curious about how it feels to be a Negro. Maybe I shouldn't even notice that most of the people I see are black or brown, but I can't help noticing and I wonder if that makes me prejudiced, which is what Mom and Dad say we're not. And even though we're best friends, I don't think I can ask Joseph about these things. I have touched his skin, though, and it feels just like mine.

I haven't forgotten about Lucrecia Mott, and I promise myself I will try to be better.

One day, Joseph and his mom have to go across the long bridge to the city of Beaufort to buy food and go to the doctor. I want to go along, and I beg to be allowed. Mom and his mom huddle and whisper and shake their heads and finally say yes, but I can tell Mom is worried. I don't know what's the big deal.

The three of us arrive in the city, and his mom parks the car on a side street. We all get out and walk toward the grocery store. People are staring, and his mom won't let me hold his hand even though we are best friends. She holds his hand, but not mine. In the grocery store, more people stare. Then Joseph decides he wants a drink of water, so we skip together to the drinking fountain in the back corner of the store. Drinking fountains. Two. A rust-stained white enamel fountain like the ones at school and a stainless steel water cooler. Joseph points to the signs. Negros. Whites. He bends over to drink from his fountain; I stretch up to drink from mine.

After the groceries are in the car, we walk several blocks to the doctor's office, which is the downstairs of a two-story house. Inside, there's a waiting room with nice furniture and a nurse sitting at a desk. Joseph's mom tells me to sit there and wait. She and Joseph go through a doorway into another room. I stand up and follow them, but the nurse says, "No, you wait here" in a kind of grumpy voice. The other people in the waiting room are staring at me. Some of them are shaking their heads. Before I turn back, I look into the other room. Everyone there is a Negro, and they are sitting on metal folding chairs.

When we get back to the island, Mom asks me how the day was. I say okay, but it isn't really fair the way Joseph and his mom are treated. She gives me a hug and says "No, it's not fair. And that's why we're here. To help make the world more fair."

It was 1955, and it still made sense that a dozen teenage children of liberal northerners could make the world more fair by painting porches and repairing window shutters.

∙ ∙ ∙

It is Christmas time and all the First-Day School kids are practicing for the Christmas pageant. I wish I could be Mary, but I never can because Jane is blond and beautiful and has a better voice for singing Away in a Manger. I am usually a cow. Occasionally an angel. The year my brother Selden is born, he gets to be Jesus in a wooden cradle with hay in it, and I stand over him, mooing and making sure he's okay. Rod is a wise man and gets to wear a crown. For people who are all concerned about fairness and world peace, I don't think this is entirely fair. Everyone should have a chance to be Mary, even if their hair is brown and they can't sing very well. I decide that next year I will protest.

The pageant takes place in the front of the Meeting room, where a bare Christmas tree sits in the corner. Beside the tree is a box of mittens all the women in the Meeting have knitted. After the pageant, we hang all the mittens on the tree, and sing *O Christmas Tree*. It looks very pretty in a wooly, sensible kind of way. I used to think the mittens were sent to children in Africa. But when I was looking at pictures of children in Africa, they were not wearing mittens or much of anything else. No, Mom says, the mittens go to poor children right here near home.

After we decorate the mitten tree, Santa comes with toys and candy canes for all the kids, and we all sing Christmas Carols for a while.

So you can see, these are not like the Quakers people think about — like William Penn and ladies in bonnets — and as I get older, I sometimes try to explain this to my friends. But it's complicated, because they all go to regular churches with preachers and communion and special prayers, and they really believe in Jesus. We talk a little bit about Jesus at First Day School, but nobody tells us what to think and honestly the older I get, the more unbelievable it all seems to me. We learn more about people in other countries, and poor people in our own country, and how we can help them, and that really all people are the same. There's a lot of talk about the inner light, and that seems to be enough.

Sometimes we just paint. One of the First Day School teachers is an artist and I don't think she knows anything about Jesus and maybe not much about the inner light. So we get to make oil paintings. I make a big one, thick with dark blue and black, with runny red splotches. Rod wants to know what it is, and I don't know. Oh, he says, I see. It's the whale and all its blood. Which now I see, of course, it is.

•••

I am thirteen. I am sitting beside Jane in Meeting for Worship, which is an hour of silent worship after First Day School. When I was small, I had to sit with Mom and Dad, but for the last couple of years I can sit wherever I want.

I don't go to meeting every week, and I don't have to stay the whole time. I know I can quietly get up and leave whenever I want. Or I can read the book I have with me. The room is silent except for the muted sound of traffic on the street in front and the occasional throat-clearing of the adult worshippers. Mom and Dad are sitting in one of the facing benches at the front and Mom sometimes glances over at me. Some women come to meeting in slacks, and some come with their blouses sloppily tucked in their skirts. But Mom always gets a little dressed up. Not too much, because people here aren't fancy. Only one woman ever wears a hat — the same one who wears purple dresses. Today Mom's wearing a light green dress with buttons up the front. Dad, of course, is wearing a suit. He always wears a suit.

I am busily counting the slats on the Meeting Room ceiling when Jane pokes me in the side. You are not to whisper in Meeting, but she leans over and says, quiet as a breath in my ear, "I have to speak".

We know, of course, that people speak in meeting when they feel moved to do so by the still small voice of God that is in every man. And woman. We have been led to believe that when God wants to speak through you, you will know it is God and the urge to share his wisdom will be irresistible. That's when the early Quakers quaked. I do not believe God is speaking to Jane. I am right beside her, and she seems quite her usual self. I shake my head at her: Don't do it.

She starts to do a little quivery thing with her hands and feet. None of the bowed heads or pensive gazes into space seem to notice. All I want is to leave. I can already feel my face getting hot with embarrassment. I open my book and pretend to read.

Jane stands up. Her long blond hair brushes against her cheeks. Like her mother, she often looks dishevelled. Just last week, on our way home from Meeting, Mom said "Not that it matters, of course, but I don't know where Sarah gets those clothes."

Everybody is looking at Jane now. Some people smile. She just stands there looking vaguely angelic. I stare straight ahead.

"God is Love" she says in a loud voice. Then she sits down.

Some years later I watched the movie *A Friendly Persuasion*, in which a young Quaker boy in Meeting for Worship leaps to his feet and makes the same startling observation.

It was too late to ask Jane where she saw the movie.

• • •

I'm trying not to stumble, but the high heels are giving me some trouble. I'm not really used to them, and Mom didn't think I should bring them, but I knew we'd be dressing up for church. Maybe she was right. Instead of making me feel grown-up, they're making me feel awkward. I hope Rob, walking beside me, hasn't noticed, because I've concluded that I'm in love with him. He's almost twenty, but everyone says I'm mature for fifteen.

It's a spring Sunday morning in inner city Philadelphia. I'm here on a weekend work camp, sponsored by the American Friends' Service Committee. Jane and I came together by train on Friday, my first trip away from home without my parents. Walking from the bus to the downtown church, where we would be staying, we had to step around garbage and we saw some men sprawled out in doorways. I think they were drunk. I hadn't seen many people drunk, nobody that drunk.

Everyone on the street was Black, which I was trying not to notice, though I wondered how that would be possible, and from the way they looked at us, I'm sure they were noticing that we weren't. I thought about Joseph and all the other black people I'd known, and just as I did when I was nine, I wondered if a really enlightened person would be blind to the difference. I'd had six years since then to become more enlightened, and still I had to stop myself from staring.

That night, the group leaders talked to us about the slum neighbourhood where we'd be working the next day, and then led a discussion about how the Inner Light propels people to action. Quakerism, we were reminded, is not just about recognizing that of God in every man. It is also about reaching out to it and meeting strangers as friends and equals. We would all be reaching out with paint brushes as we helped people freshen up their neighbourhood. *The Whale and All Its Blood* came to mind, and I wondered if paint was a particularly good medium for spreading the light.

On Saturday morning, we were assigned jobs in groups of two, and I couldn't believe how lucky I was! I was assigned to work with Rob, the only one who was not still in high school. The two of us spent all day together, painting the hallway of an apartment where a single mother lived with her three little children and an old man lay all day on a mattress without sheets. He never got up, and his room smelled awful. The paints we were using were all donated by a hardware store, and we were painting the hallway an ugly shade of green.

"I don't think we're spreading much light with this paint," I said.

"I guess nobody wanted to buy it," said Rob. "That's why it's free."

The mother tried to help us — that was the rule, the whole idea. We only volunteered with people who would work with us so we could all get to know and understand each other. But the man never got off the mattress, and the woman had to look after the kids, so we did most of it ourselves. By the end of the day, the hallway was only a little less dreary than before, but cleaner.

Rob is in college. He's already spent two years in the Peace Corps in South America. He wants to be a lawyer for poor people. He's a conscientious objector and a Quaker. We are both wearing peace pins! He likes Pete Seeger! Oh my God! We have so much in common! I've never really thought about it before, but I'm thinking I'd like to be a lawyer for poor people too.

Mom was right. I shouldn't have brought these shoes. I have to think about every step.

We are on our way to church with the family whose hallway we painted. That's part of the weekend package, part of getting to understand other people. I am wearing a blue suit with a pleated skirt and, of course, my heels. We are the object of considerable interest as we parade, in all our whiteness, along the sidewalk toward the African Evangelical Church. Inside, we sit with the woman and her children. The pew is crowded, so I am almost touching Rob. I notice that green paint still speckles my hands and is caked under my fingernails.

I have never been to an African church before, and I keep grinning, and then stop myself because I'm trying to be more sophisticated. There's shouting and singing and clapping, and the preacher calls out people by name. There are other white people from our group here with the families they've helped, and he welcomes us all and preaches about brotherly love. Then there's more singing, and a lot of people calling out "Amen"! I'm tapping my feet and wishing I could sing along, but I don't know the hymns and there are no hymnals. Also, Rob might think I was being immature.

On the way back for the group's final meal together, before leaving the city on trains and buses, I walk beside Rob, trying to get up the courage to ask for his address, wondering if he is also a little bit in love with me. I imagine going to the same university, walking through a tree-lined campus, studying law together. As we approach the church that is our home base for the weekend, he turns to me and my heart does a little flutter.

"First time in heels, I guess. You'll get the hang of it," he says.

In the train, on the way home, Jane tells me that she, too, has decided she is in love with Rob. She sat beside him at breakfast, and he gave her his address.

"I think I'm ready for a mature man," she says in her perpetually dreamy voice. She is a year older than me and knows how to walk in heels.

• • •

I'm doing homework at the dining room table when there's a knock on the front door. Dad opens it to a couple of strangers who begin by mentioning that they'd met me at the Latter Day Saints' weekly service. Well, true. My friend Judy is a Mormon, and she invited me to spend the night and go to her Sunday School and Church. It sounded interesting. "We don't believe in the Trinity," she says, setting herself and her family apart from the mainstream. It's not a subject I've given much thought to.

Her family fasts on Sunday mornings, in recognition of those who live in poverty. This is a good thing, I think, though it makes Sunday School a sort of hungry affair. The people at the church seem nice. Friendly. Not pushy. After Sunday School and church, they break their fast together with a potluck lunch.

Dad isn't rude to the couple at the door, but he does tell them that he's not interested in their spiel. Somehow, though, they manage to end up in our living room. As they begin setting up some sort of demonstration about their faith, Dad holds up his hand. He's a gentle man, but he can be firm.

"I don't need your lecture or your explanations," he says. "I have my own beliefs, but I'm not going to tell you about them. If you want to know what I believe, watch me. And I'll be watching you."

After they leave, I ask Dad if Quakers believe in the Trinity. He shrugs. Not important, he says. A distraction from what matters. We have to live in a troubled world and our job is to listen to the inner light, that still, small voice, to be as good as we can be, to live as we think right, to try to make a difference. That's all we can do.

•••

Am I still a Quaker? I don't think so. As the mother of a young family in the 1970s and 1980s, I longed for the sense of community and shared commitment that the Friends Meeting had provided for my childhood family. I dipped my toes in the local United Church, but it didn't feel right. I found a couple of other Quakers in our area, and we met for Meeting for Worship every couple of weeks for a few years—long enough to interest my daughter in Quakerism. Perhaps if there had been an active local Meeting, my spiritual evolution would have taken another direction.

As it was, by midlife I had rejected even the dogma-free tenets of the Society of Friends, convinced that the voice I heard was no more than an echo of my personal history and my own shifting perspectives. But I can't separate that history and those perspectives from childhood fantasies of slavery, from the pregnant silence of a Meeting for Worship, from an island off the coast of South Carolina, a water fountain labelled "whites", a mitten tree, and a weekend work camp in the Philadelphia slums.

I understand some of my Catholic friends who say you can reject the church, but you can never quite escape the identity. In my case, I have no interest in escaping it. Quakerism provided me with a solid foundation on which to build a principled life, a project that has never ceased to be challenging. I am grateful for it.

A section of this essay appeared in the June 2018 issue of La Presa.

V MY FATHER'S WORLD

In one of my earliest memories I am a child of perhaps four, in a small basement room that is my dad's study. Dad is at work, and I know I shouldn't be here, clambering up onto his revolving wooden desk chair. I have just overcome my fear of the desk itself, which features the carved heads of lions on both front pedestals—their open mouths and sharp teeth threatening small children—as they curve up to meet the flat, oak writing surface. That surface is cluttered with papers and a large black typewriter, but what catches my fancy are the tubes of red, pink, black, and white paint that I am just beginning to smear onto my arms when Mom comes into the room and scoots me out.

"You do not belong in Daddy's study," she says, giving me a gentle swat on the bottom. "And grease paint is not for playing. Daddy has to take those to work."

When Daddy goes to work, does he get to play with grease paint? Is that what grown-ups do?

That was when we still lived in the "little house", and when Mom regularly set a place at the supper table for my imaginary friends, Bea and George.

They were an odd pair for a four-year-old to latch onto—both grown-ups. George was a tall, thin man with glasses, sort of a stick figure who, in retrospect, resembled my dad. I don't have a clear picture of Bea, but I know she was an adult. Mostly they just followed me around, observing and commenting on my life. "That's a great picture you just painted, Paula," or "So, we're going to the grocery store again. Do you think your mom could buy Sugar Puffs?" or sometimes, "Let's play Simon Says?" which was difficult because while Bea and George were real enough to me, they didn't take turns very well, so I had to do it all myself.

I don't know if my parents worried about me. In the early 1950s, psychologists and child development specialists warned that children who indulged in such fanciful behaviour were teetering on the edge of psychological disturbance. Dr. Benjamin Spock, whose child care book was on my parents' shelf, claimed that, if a child still had an imaginary friend at the age of four "a child psychiatrist… or other mental-health counsellor should be able to find out what they are lacking." The fact that Mom and Dad welcomed Bea and George to the supper table rather than sending me to a shrink suggests they were ahead of their time. It wasn't until the late twentieth century that researchers began associating imaginary friends with intelligence and creativity, and encouraging parents to see them as a healthy part of childhood play.

For as long as I can remember, I've lived a parallel imaginary life, peopled by imaginary characters. I explain things to them, consult with them, practice conversations that I anticipate having with real people. I've never known whether this is an oddity or commonplace, or whether perhaps my father's profession as a professor of theatre arts was a contributing factor, legitimizing all manner of make-believe. Or whether, as Dr. Spock suggests, I was—am still—lacking something.

Maybe it's a family trait. Galen, my youngest child, had imaginary friends too. They didn't have names, but were simply "My two wee, wee girls", and they seemed to live in a lilac bush. I assumed they were identical twins, but I'm not sure how Galen saw them. Though miniature, they were obviously modeled on his big sister, Erica. He spoke to them often, particularly through the magical red tassel on his winter hat that dangled low enough to reach his mouth. I know he was more than four because the wee, wee girls rode the school bus with him. I think they sat on his lap while he broadcast conversations with them through the tassel.

The names Bea and George still trip along my tongue like any other well-established couple, but I don't remember much about them now. At some point between early and middle childhood, the cast of characters became more varied, invented to accommodate my immediate situation or the person I was pretending to be.

• • •

In fact, my dad's work did not focus on grease-paint. But as a professor of Theatre Arts, in a small department at Penn State University, he did find himself in the midst of all aspects of theatrical production. I think that suited him. He taught playwriting, acting, directing, stage lighting. Every year he directed at least one major production on campus. He was an avid scholar of the works of George Bernard Shaw. For several summers, he managed a local summer stock theatre. At least once a year, he and Mom took a several-day jaunt to New York City to sample the offerings on and off Broadway.

All of which is to say, my childhood and adolescence were drenched in theatrical productions and stagecraft. I assumed that bestowed on me an innate talent. And wasn't the fact that I spent much of my life pretending to be someone else supporting evidence?

I am in second grade. Mrs. Bower is talking about birds. She talks about birds a lot. I am very sleepy, and I don't really care very much about birds. I put my head down on my desk.

"Paula," she says, and I jerk awake. "Were you up late last night?"

"I was at a rehearsal," I say, puffing up a bit. "I'm in a play." I'm sure I am the only one in the class who has ever been in a play or even knows what a play is.

My dad is directing the play. It's got something to do with Japan and there are three little girls in it. We wear silky bathrobes and pajama bottoms and sit on the floor of the stage, in front of a woman who is pretending to be our teacher. She's much prettier than Mrs. Bower. We have to act out "see no evil, hear no evil, speak no evil" with our hands. I'm the hear-no-evil one so I have to cover my ears at just the right time.

Mrs. Bower doesn't think I should be in the play because it means I have to stay up late and I'm not practicing my reading or staying awake enough to learn about birds, so she has a talk with Mom and Dad. I can already read pretty well, and Mom and Dad think the play is more important than learning about birds, so I get to stay in it. And, I get special permission to come to school late some days until the play is over. On those days, Mrs. Bower always says "Well, hello Paula," in front of the whole class, like she's surprised to see me.

I don't think Mom and Dad like Mrs. Bower very much.

Dad managed to give each of his children a role in a university production. A few years after my debut, my brother Rodney played one of Medea's sons who was murdered off stage and carried back on again, dead and dripping in blood. A lot more exciting than sitting cross-legged with my hands on my ears, I thought, but Mom scolded Dad for casting her son in such a role. She had trouble seeing the blood as the runny ketchup it really was, and she cringed when Rodney practiced his death-scream in the living room.

"Relax, Mae," Dad said. "It's a great experience for him."

My much-younger brother Selden's turn came after I'd left home for college, and unlike his older siblings, he had a real role.

He played the cute, lisping child in the Music Man. He spoke, sang, and danced on stage—so much better than sitting docilely before a teacher, or lying dead and bloodied on the stage.

•••

Many adolescents dream of a life on stage or back stage. Is it the glamour? A craving for attention? The sense of community? All of that, I suppose. By thirteen, I was determined to become an actress. Again and again I tried out for parts in school and community theatre productions, and was always disappointed.

I begged Dad for acting lessons. He finally took pity when I was once again passed over for a speaking role, this time in The Wizard of Oz. Why would a person with my obvious talent be relegated to the role of a silent palace guard? So, he sat me on a straight chair in the living room and told me to watch an imaginary ladybug crawl from the back of my hand, up my forearm, toward my shoulder. The bug thing was, Dad assured me, a standard practice for acting students, and so I did it. But really, was this going to help me become an actress? I couldn't believe it. The bug reached my neck and I brushed it away.

When he assigned me a long speech from *Androcles and the Lion*, I poured my heart into it. As I recited it with great emotional flair, he nodded quietly and when I finished, he cleared his throat and said, "Well, gal, that was a good bit of memorization."

Despite Dad's lack of enthusiasm, I was determined to imbibe that potent cocktail of camaraderie, fantasy, and hard work that was the theatre. He opened the door an inch by giving me a job at Standing Stone Playhouse. For several summers, he managed the summer stock theatre, an old barn converted to a theatre-in-the-round, in the Allegheny mountains half an hour out of town. I ushered and worked the concession during intermissions, selling coffee, soft drinks, and bags of potato chips. I rode the cast bus to the theatre before and after performances. During the show, I lurked backstage, spending time with the professional actors and the acting apprentices. Imagining becoming one of them. Imagining I *was* one of them.

It was a dream that almost came true. The stage manager needed an extra person for scene changes. Would I be willing? It wouldn't interfere with the important work of selling potato chips.

Dressed in black, gliding across the darkened stage to remove a plate and replace it with a vase, then quietly picking up a discarded shirt before slipping out stage left—oh, the thrill of it! When Max, the director, offered me a tiny walk-on part in *Playboy of the Western World*, I was sure I was on my way. Every evening for two weeks, kerchief tied around my straight brown hair, dressed as an Irish village girl, I entered stage left carrying a roasted chicken by its legs.

"And here's a little layin' pullet I brought ye," I said in a clear voice—though never quite loud enough—holding the fowl aloft, an offer to the playboy himself. Only once was it over-roasted so that the body slid to the stage floor and I found myself holding a naked drumstick, staring down at the greasy mess beside my feet. The playboy scooped it up and carried on without missing a beat while my face burned with embarrassment beneath my makeup.

One evening before the show, I was sitting in a makeup chair inhaling the magical mixture of grease paint and cigarette smoke, watching Esther, the actress I most worshiped, apply makeup in the chair beside me.

I think she was good at her craft, but what most endeared Esther to me was the drama of her real life. She lived in sin with the director, Max. In Greenwich village, of course. Their story fed my dreams of a romantic, bohemian life. Max, I was told, had a wife in Germany who had gone mad. It was illegal — and surely inhumane — to divorce a madwoman. And so, living in sin with Esther was not really sinful in my emerging 1960s view of sexual morality. I spent much of my time imagining myself to be Esther—an actress, loving and loved by a man shackled for life to a raging maniac, turning to me for comfort and solace. Oh yes, and sex.

I gathered my courage to ask Esther, who must have found my adoration something of a burden, if she thought I could act. I still remember her careful response: "Sensitive people like you usually can act."

She wasn't about to burst my bubble.

In fact, the air leaked out slowly. The next year, I was cast as the lead in the Junior Class play, where I got to kiss my opposite number—not my choice of partners, but good practice. By the time a group of us conspired to write and produce *Macbeth, The Musical* for a school assembly (I played a witch), I had emerged from the fantasy world of stage lights and grease paint. I knew I would not be an actress. I suspect my dad heaved a sigh of relief.

•••

But what did Dad think of the real world I moved into in my mid-twenties—marrying young, abandoning academic aspirations, and devoting myself to a family farm and child-rearing, with little time for the fine arts? I don't know, can now never know. My parents had groomed me to buck the establishment, but I think they feigned enthusiasm for the way I chose to do that. I'm sure they'd imagined a different calling for their daughter. Cleaner. More refined.

As I became more focused on a physically active life, I began to realize how sedentary my childhood family had been. We didn't paddle canoes or take weekend bike rides like some of my friends' families; we went to the theatre. We spent summer vacations on the New Jersey shore, where we kids played in the surf while Dad lounged on the beach, his nose—smeared with zinc oxide to avoid sunburn—deep in a book, and Mom strolled along the sand gathering shells. We lived on a mountainside, but I don't think my parents ever climbed the well-worn paths to the top. The first time I did was at the age of thirty-five, with my own children.

Except for his annual spring enthusiasm for the vegetable garden—which had usually abated by mid-summer—my dad rarely broke a sweat. My own experience with the garden taught me to avoid, rather than embrace, physical work. Each year Dad drafted me to join him with a hoe to break up the clods of soil he had just turned over with a spade. I loathed the work, slamming the hoe angrily against the heavy soil and complaining so loudly that Dad preferred to work by himself in peace—which was, of course, my plan.

One of the first things I had to learn during our farming years was to push past my comfort zone, but I never learned to like it. I still resisted breaking a sweat, so I was never a very good farmer. Maybe I'd have been better at it if Dad had insisted I stick with the hoeing at the age of ten. Maybe if we'd donned backpacks and climbed the mountain as a family, I'd have learned to enjoy the feel of sweat dripping off my face. But nothing in my early years had prepared me to endure physical discomfort, to push myself beyond the point of exhaustion—and then to keep going until the job was done. And that, it turns out, is what farming requires. When thunder storms threatened the hay crop and we worked on the fields until dark, or when water pipes froze in the barn and we hauled bucket after bucket from the house, splashing and stumbling over frozen ground, I thought of Dad and the hoe, and I tasted the same tears of frustration and rage at the immovable forces of nature that I'd tasted when slamming that hoe against clods of dirt.

Clearly, the farming venture would have been an immediate disaster if I hadn't married a man whose attitude toward work was the polar opposite of my own.

Why? I wondered aloud as I wrote these words. Your family wasn't exactly athletic. I never saw your father do anything more physical than walk to the car.

True, he said. But they were risk-takers. Entrepreneurs. Unwilling to be defeated by a challenge.

Dad and Mom visited the farm often during those years. They accompanied us to the barn and to the sugar bush, and Dad found little projects to tackle. I was introducing them to a foreign world, and I wonder now, was he pretending to be someone else while he whistled under his breath, standing in a pile of straw and smearing glazing putty on broken barn windows?

One year, midway into our farming adventure, I decided to drive them north for a day to see the pictographs—Ojibway rock art—on Agawa Rock, on the eastern shore of Lake Superior. For some years, we had been spending the last couple of weeks of summer away from the farm, camping in Lake Superior Provincial Park. I wanted to share the beauty of that place. I knew, of course, that my parents weren't wilderness types. But they were art-lovers. Dad had recently left the Theatre Department to develop a multidisciplinary arts program for undergraduates. I knew he would be fascinated by these rock paintings. I pictured him gazing in awe at an art form he'd never seen before, imagined him including a unit on rock paintings in his arts program, maybe with attribution. *I'm grateful to my daughter for introducing me to these unique aboriginal paintings...*

As I laced up my sturdy hiking boots before leaving home, I glanced at Dad's smooth leather oxfords and Mom's somewhat more sensible sneakers.

"It's a bit of a hike, Dad. Do you have other shoes?"

He didn't.

"These will be fine, Paula. I'll put my toe-rubbers on."

Two hours later, I was leading the way down the rocky descent to the water's edge, more rugged than I'd remembered. I kept looking back at Dad. His toe-rubbers kept him from slipping on the rocks, true, but his gait was hesitant, unsteady. Mom wasn't having any trouble, but she was staying close by him. We were going downhill toward the lake shore; the return would be more difficult.

"This is much more than we usually do, Paula," Mom said.

"It gets worse. But it's really worth it, I promise." Truth is, I was beginning to worry, too. On the way to the water, we stopped to read the signs explaining the paintings and their significance to Ojibway culture.

It was a shining fall day. Sunlight twinkled off the dark ripples of the lake as we approached the steep cliff face with the narrow, sloped stone ledge that allows viewers to inch along the sheer rock face to view a dozen reddish-brown pictographs—painted in ochre by the local Ojibway, standing on this same ledge hundreds of years ago. A magical place. A place to imagine another time, another life. A place I wanted my dad to love.

Mom and Dad exchanged terrified looks. I led the way, leaning against the slope to keep my balance. Mom crept a few yards along the ledge before announcing she'd seen enough. Dad didn't venture out at all. I choked back tears as we trudged up the trail to the car.

I chide myself still for not knowing Dad better. In my eagerness to play out a scene that had captured my imagination, I forced him to reveal his limitations. I know, now, how hard that is for parents. It's one thing to try to shove the square pegs of my imagination into the round holes of my own reality and another to cast the show with characters from real life, only to be disappointed when their edges are too sharp to slip into place.

Dad was not failing. He was a healthy man in his sixties who enjoyed his daily stroll, but was unaccustomed to rocky hiking trails. And I, much like the four-year-old who set the table for Bea and George, had let my imagination rule the day. Dad and I had a decade left together, and I'm sure that day's misadventure did not dominate his memories. But like me, I doubt he forgot it either.

Bea and George did no one any harm. Neither did the flights of imagination that cast me in a variety of leading roles throughout my life—the vast majority of which bore little relation to the reality of my unfolding world. I can't be sorry for all the places my imagination has taken me in my nearly eight decades, all the people it's allowed me to be. It's brightened my life when things were not going well. It's prepared me to face a variety of possible futures, some of which have unfolded in real life. It's allowed me to experience vicariously things I would never experience in fact.

Dad invited me into his world, a world that encouraged my flights of fancy. He also taught me, that day on Lake Superior, that free-wheeling imagination needs be reined in when the supporting actors have trouble following the script. Thanks for both, Dad.

VI THANK YOU FOR THE PIES

It is January, 2000. I am sitting on one of the facing benches at the front of the Quaker Meeting House. A fire crackles in the fireplace, an attempt at coziness. Beside me sits my husband Jack; just beyond him, on the same pew, my two brothers and their wives. Most of the pews are filled, many with faces from my childhood, aging but still familiar. Only my dad is missing; sixteen years ago I sat in this same spot, grieving for him.

Across the room, a younger man I don't recognize stands, clears his throat, and speaks into the silence.

"I will miss Mae for many reasons," he said. "Not least, I will miss her pies. Even when she knew she had little time remaining, she volunteered pies for this year's silent auction. Her pies have found their way into the hearts and stomachs of most of us here. Pies were one of Mae's many ways of telling us how much she cared. We will miss her caring."

He cleared his throat again, hesitated as though to speak more, and sat down. I stared down at my hands and gathered my courage. Both of my brothers had spoken. The only rules here were unwritten, but I knew them well. It was my turn. As I began to rise, Jack reached over and squeezed my hand.

"My mother gave me many gifts. Alas, pie-making was not one of them." My voice quavered, and I paused to calm myself. "At each stage of my life, she set an example for how to navigate the next stage. When I was thirty, she was showing me how to be fifty. When I was forty, she showed me that sixty was nothing to be afraid of. She moved gracefully from mother to grandmother, and from homemaker to professional woman. All with energy and enthusiasm." I swallowed hard and continued.

"Of course, I'd like to have a longer life than she had. But if I don't, as a final gift, she has shown me how to face that too." My voice was failing me. "I will miss her. And her pies."

∙ ∙ ∙

I should have mastered the art of pie-making at my mother's knee; I witnessed it often enough. But by the time I was old enough to become an apprentice in the kitchen, I fancied myself above such domestic drudgery. By then, too, Mom was beginning to veer away from her 1950s wife-and-mother persona, but as the speaker at her memorial service noted, she never stopped baking. Cakes, muffins, pies. Especially pies. Apple, pumpkin, cherry, berry — and crumb pies.

Crumb pie—that Pennsylvania Dutch specialty more commonly known as shoo-fly pie. Both names are descriptive in their own way, but crumb pie never sat around long enough in our house to attract flies. It is, I am told, an acquired taste, but we all acquired it as toddlers so I've never understood how anyone can turn their nose up at that molasses-sweetened cake-like filling with sugary crumbles on top.

My first adult attempts at pie-baking, in my mid-twenties, coincided with my health-food craze. This was not a good match. Whatever you may read about the excellence of pie crusts made from whole grain flour and soy oil, do not be deceived. If you want to celebrate whole grains and unsaturated oils, consider muffins or pancakes. If you crave a pie with a tender, flaky crust, you will have to sacrifice your whole-food principles. During those years, when I was feeding blackstrap molasses to my infant son and whipping up batches of Adele Davis's Tigers Milk, I abandoned the pie-making enterprise.

And yet, pies continued to occupy a place of honour in the comfort food corner of my brain. Macaroni and cheese. Roast beef with Yorkshire pudding. Campbell's bean with bacon soup. Sponge cake. Sauerkraut on mashed potatoes.

Later, when I moved to the country, pie crusts assumed an even greater symbolic significance as I tried to integrate a principled commitment to natural food with my newly acquired identity as a northern Ontario farm wife. Pies were everywhere—by the slice on small paper plates at country auctions, sold whole in aluminum pans to raise money for charitable causes, donated for community suppers, and served warm from the oven at the neighbour's kitchen table.

Contrary to my assumptions, mistakenly cultivated by *Harrowsmith* and *Organic Farming and Gardening*, most farm folk were not health food aficionados. They grew their own vegetables and ate their own meat, sure, but they didn't offer up unsweetened berries in a wholesome brown crust for dessert. No. If they raised pigs, they rendered their own lard. If not, they bought Tenderflake. Possibly Crisco. Sugar flowed freely, and if, by some remote chance, they had whole wheat flour in their pantry, they knew better than to use it for pie crusts.

At the same time as I was trying to establish my credibility as a country woman, I was trying to become a Canadian. The two identities merged in butter tarts, a Canadian specialty that does not appear in any health food cookbook on earth, consisting as it does of butter, sugar, corn syrup, and egg baked in a melt-in-your-mouth crust. Clearly, before I could take the oath of citizenship, I had to master butter tarts. Which meant learning to make pie crust.

Eventually, I settled on a recipe called "no-fail pie crust"—featuring margarine, egg and vinegar—which, as promised, never failed to yield an easy-to-roll, somewhat rubbery dough and a passable, though not flaky, baked crust. That's what I used for holidays or when required to donate pies to local community suppers. It was good enough.

Until the spring of 2000. That's when I inherited Mom's slate pie-crust slab and with it, the urge to master the traditional art of pie crusts. Sometime in the late 1960s, after I had left home, this eighteen-inch round, silky-smooth surface, made from slate harvested from the quarries of her hometown in eastern Pennsylvania, replaced the pastry cloth Mom had used for rolling out pie crusts and cookies when I was a little girl. Its dense, perpetually cool surface prevents the dough from sticking. It now hangs in my kitchen, and I never use it without thinking of her.

•••

The sun casts shadows from the bare elm tree outside the kitchen window onto the pine kitchen table, where Mom is using two knives to cut up lard and flour into little pieces. I am standing on a chair, watching the knives go back and forth, clicking like a wind-up clock.

"Now," says Mom, and I sprinkle cold water on, just a tiny spoonful at a time, until she says "Stop!"

She pushes her brown hair away from her forehead, leaving some flour stuck to her face.

"You're dirty with flour!" I say.

She laughs and puts a dab of flour on my face, too. "Let's get this show on the road."

That's what she says whenever it's time to do something. This time, it's making the crumb pies for tomorrow's dinner. Thanksgiving.

She squeezes the dough into a ball and pats it flat on a stiff piece of cloth that has flour all stuck into it, then picks up the rolling pin, which is wrapped in a special knitted sock.

As I conjure up this memory of 1950s pie-making, and the image of the pastry cloth and rolling pin cover come clearly into view, I realize that I have never used a pastry cloth or a sock for my rolling pin. I'm not sure I've ever seen them outside my mother's kitchen.

"Can I try?"

Mom moves my chair a little closer to the table and puts the rolling pin in my hands. Then, she puts her hands on top of mine and we push the dough bigger and flatter. When it's big enough, Mom folds the raggedy-round piece of dough in half two times so it comes to a point, then lifts it into the pie pan with the point in the middle and unfolds it so it covers the whole pan. With a sharp knife she cuts around the edges to make them even. Strips of crust drop away from the pan onto the cloth. I nibble on their stiff, slightly salty goodness while she fancies up the crust edges. I can't take my eyes off her hands. Her fingers know just how to pinch the edges so they look like the rickrack on the edge of my red nightie. The white tip of her fingernail pokes in and out of the crust, and her wedding ring is wobbly on her ring finger.

After the crust edges are all pinched, she mixes flour, sugar, and butter in the big brown mixing bowl to make the crumbs. She stirs eggs in another bowl, and then adds molasses and hot water.

She hands me the molasses spoon to lick. "That'll sweeten you up!"

"Now, watch this," she says, and stirs in a tiny bit of baking soda from the square orange box. The whole bowl bubbles up and almost overflows. She pours some of that foamy stuff into the crust to make a puddle, and I help sprinkle the crumbs on top until the puddle is gone. We do it again and again until the pie pan is full.

Then I gather up the rest of the dough scraps and put them in my own little pan. I sprinkle sugar and cinnamon on top and Mom puts them in the oven with the pies. Pie crust cookies!

•••

It is 1956, another Thanksgiving. The turkey is in the oven and the whole house smells warm and happy. The pies—apple, pumpkin, crumb—are lined up on the kitchen table. The kitchen windows are steamed up, and every time anyone opens the kitchen door a cold wind rushes in, along with some dry leaves.

Dad is putting up the storm windows because it's Thanksgiving morning and that's his job. My brother Rodney is outside with him.

Mom is wearing an apron that goes over her dress like a big blouse put on backwards and tied at the back. I am sitting at the kitchen table decorating napkins with coloured pencils. That's been my holiday job since I was about three, before I could trace the swirly lines on the napkins. After the napkins are finished, I will also print out a place tag for everyone who's coming: Grammy Smith, Aunt Sarah, Uncle Ray, and Aunt Florence. And, of course, there's Mom and Dad, me and Rodney. Selden is just a baby so he doesn't get a place at the table.

Selden is in a little bouncy chair beside me, and another of my jobs is to bounce him if he starts to cry.

"When will they get here?" I ask.

"They'll get here when they get here," Mom says—which means "Can't you see I'm busy?"

She is pulling the round oak dining room table in half so she can put the leaves in to make it long and oval. I watch from the doorway, holding the napkins and name tags at the ready. But she's having trouble pushing the table back together. She gives the end a kick with her foot and stubs her toe.

"Darn it anyway."

That's the foot and the voice she used last week when she kicked the dog, Frisky, out of the kitchen after he ate the roast that was defrosting on the counter. And then, when she slammed the door hard behind him and the window broke, she said "Damn!"

Today, she gets Dad to help push the table together, so there's no disaster, and he says, "Just relax, Mae," but I can tell she isn't relaxing. I've started noticing that she doesn't really like having all of Dad's family here, but she has to pretend.

She spreads a gold-coloured tablecloth on the long table top. Then I help her spread the lace one that Grammy Smith made on top so the gold shows though the lace. We always use the lace tablecloth when Grammy comes for dinner. I help Mom spread it. Then, the plates—not the usual grey Boontonware but the special white dishes we use for fancy meals.

At last. On each plate, I carefully arrange a decorated napkin so it's sitting in a diamond shape in the middle, and at each water glass I fold a place tag in half so it stands up.

When Dad comes in, he looks at the table and says it looks very nice…but it's not a good idea to have Aunt Sarah sitting beside Aunt Florence, and Rodney should sit beside Mom, and I should sit beside him, and he moves all the nametags around even though he isn't helping with dinner at all.

When the car full of relatives finally arrives, Dad helps Grammy Smith out of the car and says *"Wie Gehts*, Mom." Uncle Ray and Aunt Sarah get out of the front seat, and Aunt Florence gets out of the back. She is Dad's oldest sister and lives in New York City. Everybody hugs everybody else and says how the traffic was awful and how there was snow coming over the mountain and how it's been too long.

Selden is just a few months old and very cute, so he gets passed around until he starts screaming and they give him to Mom. As soon as he's quiet, she gives him to Grammy so she can make the gravy and mash the potatoes. Grammy and Dad go into the living room where they start talking Dutch, which isn't really Dutch. Dad says it's Deutch for German, but it isn't really German either, but Pennsylvania Dutch. So it *is* Dutch.

The kitchen is warm with cooking and talk, and I try to listen to everything the grownups are saying. Aunt Sarah and Aunt Florence are arguing about how much butter to put on the peas and the corn and whether there should be one bowl of stuffing or two, and whose fault it is that they forgot the bring the chow-chow, and should we have bread on the table with so much other food. Their large, soft, bustling bodies wrapped in floral dresses and smelling of soap fill the kitchen and push Mom to the edge. She is mashing the potatoes, and beside Aunt Sarah and Aunt Florence, she looks small. I can't see her face, but I know if I could, her lips would be squeezed together like when she's mad, but I don't think she's mad, not really. It's just what Aunt Sarah and Aunt Florence do to her.

Finally, everything is on the table. The turkey is on a big board at Dad's place. While everyone looks for their place tag and sits down, Mom makes sure they know that I made the place tags and the napkins. Then Dad says, "Shall we have a moment of silence?" That's how we say grace at our house, and because it's Thanksgiving it's more like two moments.

Finally, Dad raises his head.

Right away, Aunt Sarah says, "Well, I'll never get used to this Quaker way of doing things, Warren."

"You never did see much use for other people's ideas, did you Sally?" says Aunt Florence from across the table.

"Flo, you know that's not true. I know you don't go to church anymore now that you live in the big city. You probably just don't remember how to pray properly."

Flo's turn. "I guess Warren can do what he wants in his own house."

"Okay, Sis," says Dad, looking from one to the other. "A little silence is not a bad thing." He's using the same voice he uses when Rodney and I fight and I kind of get why he moved their place tags.

Their own mother, Grammy Smith, hardly ever says anything but she's shaking her head. I think she likes Dad best.

Then Dad stands up at his place and begins to carve.

And now this childhood memory is overtaken by the memory of another, more recent dinner. It is Thanksgiving Day, 1983. I have made a trip back to my parents' home, still my childhood home, with my husband Jack and our three children. My brothers are there, too—Rodney and Selden with their partners; it is a rare gathering of the whole family. Of those earlier guests, only Aunt Sarah remains and she is not with us on this day. The same oak table—enlarged by its leaves and covered with the lace tablecloth—is laden with all the trimmings. The cranberry sauce sparkles, translucent in its cut-glass bowl; the mashed potatoes heap high beside the stuffing and gravy; the peas and corn add colour at opposite ends of the table. I know there are pies in the kitchen.

From an invisible chalice, as large as the room, grief spills over everything.

Dad sits at the head of the table. He has always insisted that a round table has no head, but today it's oval and he is at the end near the window. Two pale plastic tubes emerge from his nostrils, tethering him to an oxygen tank on the floor by his chair. He asks for a moment of silence, as he has every Thanksgiving I can remember. In that quiet, my eyes fill with tears that overflow and trickle down my cheeks. Mom blows her nose, and Jack reaches for my hand.

Dad stands for a moment, looking down at the Thanksgiving turkey, browned to perfection, then around at his family. He is unbearably thin.

"Another feast, Mae," he says to Mom, as he always does. "We've a lot to be thankful for."

He picks up the carving knife and the two-pronged meat fork—then puts them down and turns to his oldest son. In a raspy voice, he says, "Rodney, would you carve?"

I suppose the pies were as plentiful, their crusts as succulent as ever on that day.

• • •

I'm afraid that, if my mother were here to read these words, she would express dismay. "Is this really how you think of me, Paula? As a maker of pies, a cooker of family dinners, a kicker of dogs? Am I stuck forever in the kitchen for you?"

And I would not know what to say. What child really understands the continuing evolution of her parents? What parent can program the images her child carries into adulthood?

And so, yes, Mom. I'm afraid so. Perhaps not the dog. That, to my knowledge, happened only once, and god knows you were justified. But you did have a door-slamming temper. Surely you wouldn't deny that? You were "spunky", as Dad would say, shaking his head.

But the pies? That's more complicated.

When I cast back to my childhood, I try to see you reading, studying, becoming politically and socially active. I know that you were doing these things. By the time you were in mid-life, growing into the person you would become, I was observing you from afar, growing into the person I would become. When an older woman gave you a shawl that had belonged to Susan B. Anthony, saying you were the most deserving of her friends, I shook my head in amazement.

But when you come to me unbidden, you are not in a meeting or an office, or on a protest line. You are not in the mold of Susan

B. Anthony. You are in the kitchen. Sometimes I am small, standing beside you on a chair stirring pudding in the copper-bottomed saucepan or cutting out Christmas cookies. Sometimes I am an angry adolescent, venting rage as you insist that I dry the dishes. Sometimes I am an adult, and we have been drawn to the kitchen—yours or mine—to be nourished by the many tasks and confidences women share in kitchens.

In one of those moments, sometime between Dad's final Thanksgiving and his death, I asked, "Will you be okay. Alone?"

You paused, on the verge of some revelation, squared your shoulders and fixed your blue eyes directly on mine. "Let me show you something." Your voice was clear. Determined.

You opened an upper cupboard, pulled a kitchen chair over to reach the top shelf, and took down a few dishes. A single place setting—dinner plate, salad plate, soup bowl, cup and saucer—fine china in a delicate shade of blue with a gold rim. Unlike anything else in the cupboard. Finer than any dinnerware you'd ever owned. You placed them on the counter and fingered them gently.

"I bought these at an auction six months ago, when I knew I would be alone. Dinner for one." You paused again. "Dad doesn't know about them. He doesn't have to."

I nodded.

I never saw those dishes again. But I have imagined you, sitting at the dining room table alone, perhaps with a single candle reflecting in the window against the dark of a winter night, perhaps with Susan B. Anthony's shawl draped over your shoulders, enjoying dinner for one. Perhaps, before your first bite, you hear Dad's voice asking for a moment of silence.

• • •

The year after Dad's death, Mom spent Thanksgiving with us.

During the 1970s and 1980s, the holiday became a true harvest feast for our family, the culmination of the farming and gardening year. Never mind that our back-to-the-land endeavours often ran amok; our Thanksgiving table was always laden with food produced and prepared by our own hands. A turkey, raised from a small chick, its initial cuteness long forgotten; potatoes dug from our own garden soil; carrots, peas, cabbage, squash, stored or frozen from the summer's harvest; high-bush cranberries gathered from the river's edge; pumpkin pies from our own pumpkins smothered in whipped cream from our own cow, in a crust prepared from our own rendered lard.

"You make the pie crusts, Mom. You're the expert." I handed her the lard and pointed to the canister of flour.

Her response stunned me. "Oh, Paula," she said. "I never make pie crusts from scratch anymore. I use Mrs. Smith's Pie Crusts. You just unfold them, roll them a bit, and put them in your own pie pans. They're as good as mine. And after all, I am Mrs. Smith."

•••

The twentieth century is in its final weeks. At Mom's request, the whole family has gathered for Thanksgiving: children, grandchildren, great-grandchildren.

Tomorrow's meal is being catered, but Mom is determined that the pies will come from her own small kitchen, a tiny replica of that kitchen where the elm tree's buds, leaves, and bare branches announced the passing of seasons, years, generations.

"Now you want to stir the pumpkin into the eggs, milk, and sugar."

Yes, Mom, I know how to bake pies now, too. I silence that inner adolescent. This is her last production, so I hold my tongue and follow orders.

We two are alone, my mother and me. The slate slab sits on the table, flour-coated. Crusts are in the pans, edges crimped, awaiting their fillings. With a wink in my direction and a weak smile, Mom has buried the Mrs. Smith's Pie Crust boxes in the trash.

"No one will know," she says.

"Nor care," I say. And yet, oddly, I do.

I pour the pumpkin mixture into one shell and fill another with apple slices. While Mom sits at the table weaving a lattice top over the apples, I layer the contents for the crumb pies, then slide them all into the oven.

The familiar smells of cinnamon, molasses, and bubbling apples soften and enlarge the unfamiliar kitchen, and for a moment, I am sure I hear Dad banging the ladder against an outside wall as he prepares to hang the storm windows. Mom is mashing potatoes beside the harvest-gold stove; my brothers are stealing cookies from the plate on the counter; the aunts are crowding the room with their plump, argumentative selves.

But no. On this November afternoon, it is just Mom and me, sharing a moment that we both know will not come again. We could have reminisced over family photos. We could have sipped tea and talked about her grandchildren and her great-grandchildren. We could have put into words the unspoken feelings of a lifetime.

We baked pies.

> Mae Spangenberg Wilson Smith
> 1925-2000.

VII THE UNSPEAKABLE

Most girls first menstruate when they're about thirteen. Some begin when they're only ten years old...
　　　　　　　From "How Shall I Tell My Daughter", Modess, 1954

"I have periods now...I too am among the knowing, I too can sit out volleyball games and go to the nurse's for aspirin and waddle along the halls with a pad like a flattened rabbit tail wadded between my legs..."
　　　　　　　Margaret Atwood, *Cat's Eye*

The crackling sound of a paper bag unfolding in the dim corner of my bedroom closet echoes through the house. I reach in and extract a pad and an elastic belt—more like a harness, really, with hooks on both ends. Awkwardly, I scrunch the pad between my legs and attach its gauzy ends to the hooks, change my underpants for the third time, and bury the soiled underwear deep in the laundry hamper. On the floor of my closet, the cover of "Growing Up and Liking It" mocks me with a smiling, blond fifteen-year-old, wearing a crisp blue shirtdress with puffed sleeves, leaning against a white pillar surrounded by rosebushes.

　　I am not that girl.

● ● ●

Even if we lived in a culture that celebrated this coming of age event, my own arrival on the cusp of womanhood might have passed under the radar, coming as it did just hours after my mother had given birth to her long-awaited third child. And we are not such a culture. We celebrate getting a driver's license, graduating from high school, and our first drink in a bar. But the intricate workings of our young girls' maturing bodies continue, even sixty-five years later, to be subjects of hushed conversation—despite the now-widespread advertisements of "feminine products". I have no recollection of my own daughter's first period, nor does she, which suggests it was neither traumatic nor celebratory. I have granddaughters now. We shall see.

For me, that July day in 1956 began with the news of a new brother and, of more immediate interest, the chance to ride a horse. Ever since I had learned to climb the apple tree in our front yard, I had imagined myself an equestrian, wild and free. I hung stirrups made of rope from my horizontal saddle-branch and attached reins to the barky equine neck which curved elegantly upward from the saddle toward my horse's leafy head. For hours, I rode into and through imagined worlds inhabited by beings who recognized my charm and talents that had so far gone unnoticed in the real world.

On that morning, I lined up with other neighbourhood kids for a turn riding a real horse, thanks to a local teen offering free rides on her brown and white steed. As I rode up and down our mountainside road, my imagination spiraled out of control. I would own a horse; it would be black; my parents would let it live in the garage; maybe they'd even build me a little barn. I would ride across the pastures behind our house, and into the woods, a beautiful young woman in a magical world.

When, too soon, I had to give up my turn on the horse to another eager child, I went into the house, into the bathroom, and there it was.

Dad was just home from welcoming his new son into the world.

"I need to talk to Mom," I muttered.

"What's up, gal? You know she's in the hospital. You have a new baby brother!"

I glared at him. "I know that. I need to talk to Mom."

Maternity wards were not easy places to reach by phone in those days. An hour later, I was finally talking to my mom. She told me about the new baby. I knew about that. I didn't care. I had my own sorry tale to tell.

"It might have just been the horse," I say.

Mom did not think so and reminded me of the package of "supplies" in my closet. "Remember, I showed you how to use them. I'll be home in a few days, and Grammy's coming tomorrow. You'll be fine, Paula."

I was only ten, and I was not fine.

Two generations later, having played all roles in this little drama—distraught pre-teen facing puberty too early, mother of newborns, and mother of a pubescent daughter —I marvel at the unfortunate convergence of events.

•••

Still crouched in the closet, I take another look at the girl in the blue shirtdress and throw the pamphlet across the room. I wipe my eyes, and try to walk downstairs normally.

"What's the matter with you?" asks Rodney.

"Nothing. Shut up."

The typewriter in Dad's study pauses, and he emerges to give me a quick hug. "It's all quite natural, gal. You're growing up." Mom must have told him.

I pull away and stomp out of the house in search of my imaginary kingdom. Dad goes back to his typewriter.

The next afternoon, my Grammy arrived to take over the household until Mom came home with the new baby. A week-long hospital stay after giving birth was normal in those days. Grammy insisted on taking me along to Murphy's, the local five and ten store, to purchase my own box of sanitary napkins. The moment is etched into my memory — perhaps slightly embellished as befits the event.

We stood just inside the heavy glass doors, breathing in the smells of the ancient, unfinished wood floor and stale popcorn. To our right, the lunch counter was packed with shoppers drinking coffee and cokes and eating hamburgers.

I cringed as Grammy approached the nearest employee, an adolescent boy. A boy! From her enormous purse, a megaphone materialized and drifted of its own accord toward her face: "Where are the sanitary napkins?" she blared, suddenly assuming the dimensions of a giantess with dyed red hair and a hooked nose. As one, the lunch-counter customers swiveled on their stools to stare. I cowered behind a rack of school supplies.

The confused lad pointed her to an aisle containing paper plates and table napkins. "No," she shouted into her loud speaker. "Not table napkins. *SANITARY NAPKINS.*"

At that point, an older female employee, no doubt startled by the gigantic woman screaming about the unspeakable, approached Grammy. I hid my face in a giant green three-ring binder, but Grammy took me firmly by the arm as the woman quietly led us to the appropriate aisle.

"Might as well get you another belt too," Grammy continued to shriek. "They do get soiled sometimes."

The employee turned and gave me a sympathetic smile. She patted me on the back. "Growing up, are we? You'll be fine," she said in a normal voice. I wanted her to hug me. I wanted to go home with her. Instead, I went home with my Grammy — who had resumed her normal size and demeanor by the time we reached the car — and my very own box of pads in a brown bag.

By the time Mom completed her hospital stay and came home with baby Selden, the soiled evidence of my impending womanhood had found its way to the garbage and I was pretending it had never happened.

Probably caused by the horse.

Except, of course, it wasn't. I entered the sixth grade at Lemont Elementary School as the only menstruating girl, save one who had been held back a year, and so was a year older. A few other girls were wearing bras — double A.

One day, the school nurse sent all the boys out of the room and showed a movie, featuring a saccharine female voice explaining a diagram of the female reproductive system and the same self-confident teenager in the shirtdress who graced the front of the booklet. Now everyone knew that eventually they, too, would "fall off the roof", "get the curse", "get company". They probably thought they'd soon be lounging against a white pillar surrounded by rosebushes. I was the only one who really knew.

I suppose I could have been the subject of envy if I'd known how to play my cards. Woman of the world. But I was a somewhat pudgy, self-conscious ten-year-old whose precocious physical maturity had curved her shoulders downward, prompted an eruption of pimples on her face, and required her to hide sanitary pads in the brown leather binder with her homework.

"Why are you taking your notebook to the bathroom?"

"Um, stuff in it..."

I was not a woman of the world. Not then. Not ever.

• • •

So much happens when a girl reaches her teens. It's the time in your life when you first know the thrill of buying your own clothes. When you wear make-up and nail polish for the first time. When you start going to parties and dances and have your very first "date."

But, with all the fascinating things that happen in your teens, chances are, like most girls, you've run into a few puzzling problems, too.
From "Growing Up and Liking It", Modess, 1957

By the time I was in junior high, almost everyone was falling off the roof, and the girls' rooms were equipped with dispensers to catch them before they hit the ground. I no longer had to sneak into a stall and hope no one could hear me fumbling, or wait for the washroom to vacate before approaching the garbage can.

To my great relief, many girls were out-developing me, proudly flaunting their womanly figures in matching sweater sets. That's what the Popular Girls wore in 1957, along with pleated wool skirts just below the knee, ribbed bobby socks twisted into a spiral around their ankles and lower calves, and saddle shoes. Their teased hair stayed puffy right through the day, and they knew, somehow, which boys were cute. Those very boys asked them to jitterbug during lunchtime. I wanted to be like them, but I didn't know how.

I didn't actually know any Popular Girls, but I sat beside one in Art Class. Her name was Ruth. She had blonde hair and her bobby socks never sagged. Once, I gathered up all my courage and asked her, "What would I have to do to be Popular? And to get boys to like me?" One would surely follow the other.

She shrugged. "Well, maybe you should wash your hair more often. And get some Clearasil." She brushed her own fluffy locks away from her smooth cheeks and I imagined myself blond and flawless.

There was nothing I could do about the blond part, but I began applying Clearasil every morning, covering the red spots with an unnatural shade of beige. I shampooed every second day and slept in brush rollers that hurt my scalp. Still, the Popular Girls didn't invite me to sit with them at lunch, and when I overheard them giggling and oohing over cute boys in the school cafeteria, I wondered how they could tell which ones were cute? What was wrong with me, that I didn't just know?

One day, when I walked into Art Class, Ruth was standing with a group of girls in the back of the room. She called me over. I thought maybe they were going to include me in some secret or invite me to get a coke with them after school.

They opened a spot for me in their circle and I stood between Ruth and another girl whose name I didn't know. Ruth spoke.

"Hi Paula. Hey — this is a test. Look at your fingernails."

"Okay." I bent my fingers toward me in loose fist. They didn't notice the bitten nails or the ravaged cuticles. That's not what they were looking for. They just looked at each other and snickered.

"That's how guys do it," said Ruth. "Girls do it like this," She bent her palm forward and her wrist back to reveal a graceful hand with a mood ring on one finger and five smoothly rounded nails.

The incident sent my thirteen-year-old brain into overdrive as I began to put it all together. Something was wrong with me. I wasn't popular because I wasn't very feminine. I was a little plump. My hair and my skin didn't shine. My socks drooped, no matter what I did. My mohair sweaters pilled. I wasn't sure whether the boys I thought were cute really were cute; in fact, the one I liked best was short and wore glasses, which was probably wrong. And now, it seemed, I looked at my fingernails like a boy.

Two weeks later, Health Class—girls only—featured a movie called *Boys Beware*. The antagonist was a slimy man luring an innocent boy away from the playground, taking him into an upstairs apartment, and closing the door. The screen darkened to the sound of heavy music in a minor key, and when the two emerged the man, looking more evil than before with an ugly smirk on his face, had his arm around the shoulders of the now dishevelled and ashamed-looking youngster. When one bold classmate asked, "What did they do in there?" The teacher gazed heavenward for a long moment before answering. "It's not something normal people can ever understand," she finally said. I still hear her foreign-sounding southern drawl.

I had already heard there were guys who liked other guys instead of girls. They were called "queer" and the word around school was that they wore green on Thursdays. That was one way you could tell. Would they all grow up to be like the evil man in the film? And what about the little boy? What would happen to him? The Health teacher didn't say, and no one asked.

I guessed there must be girls like that too—not very girlish, probably a bit sloppy, surely not popular. Girls who looked at their fingernails wrong. I lived in terror of the next week's movie, which we knew was entitled *Girls Beware*.

As it turned out, *Girls Beware* was not about abnormal girls shamed by the unspeakable; those girls and women would remain unidentified in my adolescent world. *Girls Beware* was about rape, also with a slimy man in the lead role, and it too faded out at the critical moment, just as the thug pushed the hysterical virgin into the bushes. But we didn't have to imagine what happened next; we had a diagram explaining what normal people did and in that respect, apparently, rapists were normal.

The diagram pulled down like a window shade in front of the blackboard and showed a naked woman and a naked man, anatomically correct but standing at a respectful distance from one another, facing forward, holding hands at the end of outstretched arms, and lacking any physical signs of passion. They gazed off into space, apparently unaware of their nakedness, while in a separate rectangle above their heads several small tadpole-like creatures hovered close to a pale pink orb with a welcoming smile on its face. In subsequent rectangles, the tadpole disappeared and the orb morphed into an ambiguous human baby born with a faint smudge where the genitalia should have been.

None of this helped me come to terms with my secret fear. I began to practice looking at my fingernails the girl-way, but it never felt natural. I tried to flirt with boys—taller ones without glasses. They didn't seem to notice.

But, as I hungrily re-read *Gone With the Wind*, I imagined myself as Scarlett or Melanie, not Rhett or Ashley, which I was pretty sure was a good sign. And in the copy of *Peyton Place* I found buried under the newspapers in the house where I babysat, I was definitely the one on her back in the sand. I had some trouble associating the sensations I experienced when reading these scenes with the couple on the pull-down diagram in health class, but I began to relax.

• • •

In time, I forgave my mother for giving birth at the wrong time, my grandmother for her megaphone, and my body for sending me down the confusing road to womanhood too soon. I forgave the Modess people for that ridiculous photo of the white pillar and the rose bushes, and the health teacher for being unable to articulate the unspeakable. But I never forgave Ruth for the months-long trauma her fingernail test unleashed.

If our culture still fails to celebrate the onset of menstruation, it does now acknowledge and celebrate a range of sexual identities. This celebration is sometimes confusing and difficult for my generation to grasp. And I'm sure it doesn't eliminate the pain—not to mention the taunting—that must accompany gender uncertainty in young people. But at least it is now something that "normal people" do understand.

In the end, my own sexual identity was not in question. But knowing, as we now do, that sexuality is not the binary thing we assumed it to be sixty years ago, I ache for those classmates who must have faced far more daunting and confusing incidents than Ruth's fingernail test. For whom their own sense of themselves was unspeakable.

Many years later, I found myself once again unsettled by fingernails. At the age of five, my youngest grandson insisted on painting his fingernails.

"I want grandma to do it!"

I balked. Not, I hasten to say, because I really cared. He was only five, and why should it matter anyway? It's just that—you know—I didn't want the other kids to tease him. The boys who don't paint their fingernails. But, with a nod from his mother, I dipped the little brush into the bottle. His fingernails were tiny and ragged, with a layer of grime beneath. He looked up at me and grinned a toothless smile.

"Even though the kids at school say pink is a girl colour, it isn't. Colours aren't boys or girls. They're just colours." And he gazed down at his grimy pink nails. The guy way.

VIII UNIVERSAL DIVIDE

According to the alphabetical seating plan in my high school homeroom, I sat directly behind Shirley Schmitt, where I could see the back of her pilled grey sweater and her matted brown hair clinging to the back of her head. I wondered if she ever washed it. I wondered why she didn't brush it. I wondered about lice.

We also shared a locker, Shirley Schmitt and I. I tried to enforce a strict division of the tiny space. My jacket hung on the left-side hook, my boots beneath it on the rust-stained metal floor, my books, notebooks, and lunch stacked on the shelf above. On her side, a worn jacket, no boots, few books, some loose papers. When I pushed my arms into my warm woolen pea-jacket at the end of the day, it smelled faintly of kerosene, the smell of poverty in the middle of Pennsylvania in the middle of the twentieth century. More than once, my lunch disappeared from the locker. Sometimes my mittens went missing. In the fall of 1960, she stole my "John F. Kennedy, He Will Win" button. It must have been her. No one else could open our locker. It was a treasure of a button; the words alternated with an image of Kennedy's face depending on the angle of vision. It cost fifty cents to buy a new one, which I transferred to my sweater before hanging up my jacket every morning.

Shirley and I inhabited different universes. I knew that she lived in a small community north of town where kerosene tanks and wood piles stood beside tar-paper clad houses. And I knew she was in the business stream. That's how it was; if you weren't going to go to college, girls prepared for business—which meant, if you weren't lucky enough to get married and have babies, you would become a secretary or a sales clerk. Maybe a doctor's receptionist.

They belonged to the Future Business Leaders of America (FBLA). Boys could be Future Business Leaders, too. Or, they could be Future Farmers (FAA).

Surely it was more complicated than that. Was there a technical stream as well? Future Welders and Mechanics of America? I don't remember. Or more likely, I never knew. Did the Future Business Leaders go on to specialize in their chosen fields? The system didn't encourage us to look below the surface.

I knew one Future Farmer. He had twin sisters in the academic stream, and I wondered what had gone wrong with their brother.

•••

In the universe of the academic stream, students were placed in English sections numbered according to ability, as measured by standardized tests. The best was Section 1; I don't remember how far it went, but there was no mystery about it. Turtles and hares. Winners and losers. I wasn't a full-fledged hare, something that plagued me throughout my high school years. Almost all of my friends were in the top section. I was in the second one—far from turtle territory, but still. I tried to convince myself it was a mistake, but it never changed for the three years I spent in that school. I moved from 10-2 English to 11-2 and, finally, 12-2. (I don't think we were sorted this way for other subjects, since I joined my hare-friends for Algebra, History, and Chemistry.)

In the locker I shared with Shirley, I once spotted her class schedule. Typing. Shorthand. Bookkeeping. 10-9 Business English. It occurred to me then that perhaps the business stream had its own turtles and hares.

•••

At the end of tenth grade, with Kennedy safely in office and the world unfolding as it should, my parents levelled an unexpected and totally unacceptable demand. I was filling out my class selections for the following year: Latin, French, English, American History, Algebra, the dreaded-but-necessary Physics, the equally dreaded but compulsory Phys Ed.

"Leave a spot for a typing class," said Mom.

I stared at her in silence. My mom had been a secretary—a very good one, my dad said with a smile whenever the topic came up. But that was years ago, and now she was the wife of a university professor. Typing and shorthand were things of her past. They had nothing to do with me.

"I don't want to. Nobody takes typing."

"You will," said Dad. I stared at him. I had expected an ally.

"Why?" My voice rose in adolescent protest. What did these people know? Why would they rip me from the comfort of my peers and thrust me into the dismal world of Future Business Leaders?

"Because typing is a skill you need to have. Whatever you do," said Dad, who was a very fast two-finger typist himself.

"I can teach myself then. And it's not just typing! It's typing and shorthand! Nobody takes shorthand. Nobody."

"It won't hurt you a bit," he said. "It'll come in useful in college. Ask your mom. She can take notes at the speed of light," he said, with a wink in her direction.

"She never even went to college. How would she know?"

"That's enough, young lady." I had ventured onto the thin ice of my mother's insecurities, and Dad would have none of it. "You will be taking a typing class. If it includes shorthand, so be it. And I very much doubt you'll be the only person who does."

Typing met right before lunch. MJ, Cathy, and Linda waved a cheerful goodbye as we all left physics class. They hefted their books and binders onto their hips and turned right toward the study hall I'd sacrificed in order to learn secretarial skills. I sighed and turned left toward the Business Wing, joining the flow of Future Business Leaders of America. Two girls going up the stairs ahead of me were deep in conversation about an upcoming weekend party and who they'd be going with, their short, straight skirts just touching the crease at the backs of their knees as per school dress code. They seemed oddly content as they made their way toward a meaningless life.

In front of them, the familiar, slouching back and unkempt coif of Shirley Schmidt turned into the typing room alone. I followed her in and silently took my seat, rolling a piece of paper into place and opening my typing binder to the day's exercises. I started typing a business letter to a mattress company that had failed to deliver its order to a retail store. Tap, tap, tap, I tried not to look at my fingers. Shirley shuffled through some papers on her desk and snuffled loudly. We rarely spoke; I still remembered the Kennedy button. I looked over and saw smudges of mascara like bruises around her eyes and tears running down her face. At that moment, I vowed I would never wear mascara.

"What's the matter?" I asked. As seatmates, we had established a speaking relationship.

"Nothin'." She said. "You wouldn't understand."

"D'ya want a Kleenex?" I said, reaching into my binder and pulling out a cellophane packet. "Your mascara's running." Shirley looked at me through damp eyes.

"Yeah. Thanks." She took two tissues from the packet, wiped her eyes and blew her nose. The mascara smudge looked worse, but I didn't say anything more. The desks had gradually filled, the teacher came in, and the din of typewriter keys filled the room for the next forty minutes.

At the end of class, I watched as Shirley left the room, she and I the only ones to do so alone as the others chatted in twos and threes, making their way to the cafeteria, stopping at lockers on the way to deposit books, pick up lunch bags, meet up with friends from other classes. When I got to my locker—our locker—Shirley was there, waiting for me. Her eyes were dry, but they still had a raccoon look about them.

That never happened, except in a story I wrote about Shirley, or a character based on Shirley, in which she confided in me the details of her sad life and invited me to her home where a round kerosene heater sat in the middle of the living room. I abandoned the story before it reached a conclusion. But memory and imagination have a way of bleeding into one another, and the images I included are very clear. So I can't say with certainty that our paths never crossed outside homeroom. I can say with certainty, and belated shame, that I would not have initiated such an interaction. I was far too busy scrambling to maintain my status as a budding intellectual—a hare—to risk such a friendship.

In fact, as it turned out, Shirley would not have been in my typing class. Even there the two worlds remained strictly separated. My typing class was a dumbed-down version for the academic stream and included a "simplified shorthand" for college-bound students. I doubt the irony of that occurred to me at the time, given the weighty chip on my shoulder. Nor would it have occurred to me that not everyone *wanted* to be an "egghead", and that my cohorts and I were objects of disdain to those with a more pragmatic bent.

I never admitted to my parents how much I enjoyed typing, the rhythm and sense of control that focused on my fingertips. I still do. I wonder if Shirley and I shared that tactile pleasure.

• • •

I'm not sure when it struck me that my disregard for the less academically-inclined belied an emerging liberal worldview that focused on injustices far from home. Not in time to atone for my disregard for Shirley Schmitt and her cohorts. And not before the school instituted an "honour group" of students who, by virtue of receiving all As and Bs, were free to leave school property during their study halls. My friends and I greeted the announcement with wild enthusiasm. That is, until we learned that our phys ed marks counted. Really? How could the administration possibly justify that? Everyone knew that phys ed had nothing to do with academic success. A small group of us requested a meeting with the principal. I cringe at the memory.

"We don't think phys ed should count. It doesn't have anything to do with real education."

He begged to differ. We pressed on.

"If business students' and technical students' grades are worth the same as ours, then we should get a break for gym."

Surely I wasn't the one who said that. Surely.

I don't remember who the principal was, but from decades away I salute him. He paid us not the slightest bit of attention.

Suddenly gym class took on a new significance as I watched a cohort of successful Future Business Leaders and Future Farmers—who could not only get As and Bs, but could also climb a rope and throw a ball into a basket—trot off to the mall while I sat in study hall. The universe was tilting toward chaos.

• • •

I don't know what became of the twin sisters of the Future Farmer, but the Future Farmer himself went on to become an emergency medical technician. Oddly enough, I went on to become a farmer. And it was only then that I was forced to confront the classism embedded in my earlier worldview. Confront, yes. Acknowledge, yes. Moderate? That too. Eradicate? Who am I kidding?

In 1972, I found myself living on a farm in northern Ontario among people I would never have encountered in my ivory tower. People who had attended technical schools or studied bookkeeping instead of algebra. People who farmed, ran tourist operations, and worked in the local steel plant and pulp mills. People who could spot a snob from a mile away and eyed me and my professor-husband with caution if not downright hostility. Nobody cared that I could parse a Latin sentence or that Jack had (almost) a Ph.D. We were, well...the turtles of the farming community.

We were clueless, and the skills that had tipped the scales for us in academia weren't worth their weight in paper here. Even our collection of books about farming were of little help. What we needed were people who knew what they were doing, and it wasn't until I stood in awe as one neighbour repaired a broken hay baler, and another saved a dying calf, and yet another dealt kindly and skillfully with a disabled child whose presence made me uncomfortable, that I really began to understand the disservice I'd done to Shirley Schmitt.

Our neighbours taught us to grease farm equipment, make hay, and milk a cow. They could eyeball a woodpile and tell you how many cords were there and what you should pay for it. They didn't agree with us about politics or religion or even how to raise children, but they came to our rescue again and again with a store of knowledge and down-to-earth smarts that I had never encountered before. And yet, in spite of their best efforts, we never became more than mediocre farmers.

One day, when our friend Morley was helping repair a tractor, Jack watched, stupefied, as Morley carefully replaced one part after another. In a futile attempt to help, Jack picked up the wrong part, tried to put a square peg into a round hole. Morley turned to him and said, "You're supposed to be so damned smart, why can't you see this?"

When Jack reported this to me later, we both laughed. At ourselves. And I thought of Shirley Schmitt and the Future Business Leaders and the Future Farmers, and I whispered an apology.

The conviction that formal education bestows an unshakeable superiority eroded slowly. I'm not alone, of course. Both American and Canadian educational systems value academic pursuits over practical skills, encouraging a sense of superiority among those whose particular strengths or circumstances lead them in that direction. Educators pay lip service to the importance, even the equality, of "the trades", but they have never succeeded in convincing the academic elite, whose own egos are at stake. Even worse, I think, is the implicit assumption that those who are not comfortable expressing their thoughts do not have thoughts worth expressing.

I don't know what became of Shirley. I hope she found her niche. I hope a school system determined to humiliate her didn't do irreparable harm, and that people like me, who barely acknowledged her existence, didn't permanently damage her sense of self-worth. I think of her whenever I find myself with people whose strengths and abilities are so obviously different from my own. Then, the back of her head in homeroom comes to me, and the whiff of kerosene; she turns her head to speak, I catch a glimpse of her face, and I think perhaps I should finish that story I began.

IX WAITING FOR ARMAGEDDON

October 25, 1962. The whole world is on pins and needles, watching the showdown off the shores of Cuba. I hear the tension in the voices on the radio and in the murmur of my parents' voices just beyond earshot. The language of war: blockade, nuclear missiles, retaliation.

I saw it and heard it all day, at school, in the faces and the voices of friends and teachers. The language of fear: nervous laughter, shallow reassurances.

Now, fear has taken up residence in the dim evening of my own bedroom, pushing aside the comfort of the familiar wooden desk cluttered with schoolwork, the shabby easy chair strewn with yesterday's clothes, the metal bookshelf, crowded with university catalogues. For next year. Would there be one?

An October wind brushes the dying elm leaves against my window. I lie on my bed, staring into emptiness, trying to imagine how it would be. Would we rush terrified into the dark basement? Would we all die at once? Would there be weeks and months of pain and sickness? If I looked out these windows afterward, what would I see?

My eyes fall on a round black button attached by its pin to the border of my mirror—an inch across with a white line through the middle and an inverted arrow over the bottom third of the line. Ban the Bomb. A feeble badge of protest in a world turned against itself—the only world I've known.

I raise myself heavily to my feet, pass my younger brothers squabbling in their room—they are oblivious, I think—and walk downstairs. I cross the short hallway, past my mom, knitting and listening to the radio in the living room, and knock on my dad's study door. We always knock; it's a rule. And he always says, "Come in." He swivels in his wooden desk chair, takes off his reading glasses, rubs the bridge of his nose, and smiles at me.

"How are you, Paula?" He already knows.

I sit on the settee across from him and stare glumly at the revolving bookshelf holding the volumes that occupy his mind on better days. The eyes of his mother look down on him from a portrait hanging above his desk. Is she protecting him? Will he protect me?

"Dad, I'm scared," I choke, and suddenly the tears spill. "I'm not even seventeen. I want a chance to grow up." Then, the ultimate adolescent lament: "It's not fair."

Dad's not a demonstrative man. I don't expect a hug. But I wait for the verbal reassurance I'm sure will come. "It will be fine, Paula. They're working it out now. Relax." But it doesn't come. Instead, my dad shakes his head. When he looks up, his eyes are moist behind his glasses.

"No, it's not fair." His face assumes an expression I have never seen before. Sorrow. He can't fix this for me. We sit a long time in silence.

Two days later, the world heaved a sigh of relief as it backed away from nuclear war. Christmas came and went with its usual festivities. I finished my last year of high school and prepared to go away to university. The elm tree outside my window turned green again in the spring. And I did grow up, after all.

But I have never forgotten the look in my father's eyes when they met mine that October day and we learned together that—although a parent's love may be limitless—its power to protect is not.

• • •

I am nearing the middle of my eighth decade, and I've been waiting for the world to end for most of my life. I make plans for next week, but next year has always been iffy.

It began in the early 1950s when, as a six-year-old, I heard my parents speaking in hushed voices with each other and with their friends about the precarious state of the world. Occasionally they joined marches carrying signs saying "Ban The Bomb". I didn't know what the bomb was. I certainly had no comprehension of the geopolitical conditions that were beginning to be called a "cold war". But I knew people were worried. Even from the security of my home, in a peaceful mountain valley of central Pennsylvania—Happy Valley, they called it—I sensed the world was a threatening place.

On snowy winter evenings, I peered out the living room window into the dark, absorbing and sharing my mother's anxiety as she waited for my father's return. She pretended to dust the brick-and-board bookshelves by the window overlooking the road that wound its way up the mountainside to our house. But she wasn't prone to dusting, and she didn't fool me. I knew she was scrutinizing each set of headlights until the familiar maroon Packard station wagon turned the corner and began its final ascent—which it always did.

My playmates were oblivious to the approaching gloom. They played cowboys and Indians, cops and robbers, house, jail, school, doctor and nurse – all the childhood games that purport to mimic adult life, as though adulthood were a given. I played along, prepared to give it even odds, but I was always aware that a dark cloud floated above, subject to air currents beyond my control or understanding. No one ever wanted to play "Bomb Shelter," or "Daddy's Car Slid into the Ditch, Killing Him and Leaving Us Sad and Destitute."

• • •

My parents did not encourage me to look for dark clouds; perhaps I was hardwired to do so. In keeping with their Quakerism, they were politically progressive but personally conservative, speaking truth to power in a quiet but persistent voice, optimistic that peaceful protest and political action would lead to a better world. But in their attempt to weave together the warp of hope with the woof of indignation, they exposed me and my brothers to a confusing landscape filled with hills and valleys of fear and promise.

It wasn't until much later that I recognized the assumptions hidden within that landscape: Threats and injustices can't be ignored. You need to speak to your convictions. People can make a difference. (Oh yes, and here's the clincher that's haunted me all my life: if you don't try, the burden is yours.) And it doesn't matter what other people think.

By the time I was fifteen, I had learned to juggle those assumptions. I knew that we lived on the edge of Armageddon. I read *On the Beach* and watched *Hiroshima Mon Amour*. But, at the same time, I watched the civil rights movement in the southern U.S. take shape, and peace movements coalesce around the world, and I promised myself that I would make a difference, if nuclear holocaust didn't deny me the right to adulthood.

I also knew, as only a fifteen-year-old can, that it *did* matter what people thought. True to my deepest convictions, I wore a "ban the bomb" button—a white "crow's foot" centered on a black background. True to my need for peer acceptance, I wore it discreetly, revealing it when I felt socially safe or temporarily bold. I wanted to ban the bomb. Of course I did. I also wanted the cute boys to like me, and their personal feelings about the bomb didn't much factor into that equation. There was one boy—Raymond—who wore the crow's foot proudly, upside down: a lonely call for unilateral disarmament—the most radical position in those years of the Red Scare. He was braver than I was, and not all that cute.

•••

Recently, while poring over a drawer of memorabilia, I came upon that peace button in a small box with a couple of old political buttons and a class ring. The pin on the back is rusty now, and the button itself is smaller than I remember. Hardly large enough to make a statement.

In the same drawer, under a pile of old magazines, I found my high school yearbook. Browsing through, it's hard to tell one graduating student from another. Identically puffed hairdos and forced smiles, above necks that fade away into an indistinct blur, share space with white collars and black bowties, topped by brush cuts or Brylcreemed hair. The black-and-white photos barely distinguish the blonds from the brunettes; there were no dark skins in my high school. Alliterative descriptions accompany the faces: Cheery cheerleader keeps conversations scintillating; Mild-mannered motor mangler is mad about cars.

And then, on a right-hand page amidst the other S's, a familiar tilt of the head, wispy bangs over straight brows, eyes that stare out at me, mutely. "Thoughtful thespian hurtles through history, provides prodding and push for Piper." Is she as shocked by the aging face of her older self as I am by her pretty innocence?

Tucked between the padded yearbook cover and the front page, copies of *The Piper*, the high school newspaper, include editorials written by that thoughtful thespian, expressing lofty ideals and adolescent wisdom, social commentary and righteous indignation, occasionally hinting at the impending end of the world, and peppered with hereby's, thus's and one would think's.

And a darkened manila folder with my name—Smith, Paula Mae—typed on the tab. Inside the folder I found perhaps twenty pages, mostly typed on bond paper, a few carbon copies on onionskin. I'd obviously come upon this folder before; a post-it note was attached to the first page. "Oh dear" it said in dark ink.

"Adolescent musings." The writings are mostly poems, a several page Philosophy of Life written in a style imitating Khalil Gibran, and a two-page "autobiographical sketch"—apparently following a template provided with college application forms and ending with a passionately worded commitment to a lifetime of working toward world peace.

The poems rhyme and scan, ooze adolescent angst, and hint broadly at Armageddon. They also show not the slightest inkling of gender sensitivity. Like this one:

> To stand tall, proud, beside his life
> Is every man's desire;
> To point with meaning at his work
> Before his wits retire.
> But what man now can draw with pride
> That final, dying breath,
> When all he leaves
> To the world he loves
> Is a promise of its death.

Oh dear, indeed. And yet…the sentiment leaps across the years and finds me once again contemplating the future with dread.

• • •

Of course, protesters didn't succeed in achieving nuclear disarmament in the 1960s, nor in any of the decades since. Neither did the civil rights movement, for all its apparent successes, lead to real racial equality. But tensions eased, and my generation of North Americans relaxed into its middle years, raising our children and welcoming our grandchildren into a world of relative stability and unparalleled material comfort, unaware that our privilege and unchecked consumption were sowing the seeds for the next iteration of Armageddon—a climate catastrophe, stoked in ignorance and perpetuated by greed. Unlike nuclear holocaust, which would be—could still be—triggered by a discrete series of events, the holocaust we face now is already in motion and we seem unable or unwilling to stop it.

At the same time, the world order that has been the backdrop of my life is being shaken by extremism and threatened by a pandemic that is revealing and intensifying long-standing inequities within and between nations.

During those tense days of the Cuban Missile Crisis in 1962, when I tearfully shared my fears with my father, he could not bring himself to offer false comfort. He could only remind me that the world had tipped toward disaster before and righted itself. As I watch it tip now, I fear that it has veered to a point of no return.

The yearbook is still open. The girl with the serious eyes and the unnatural curls is still smiling at me. In some parallel universe, does she still believe she will make a difference?

"Sorry," I whisper—to her, to her children, to her grandchildren—and close the book.

Note: As I prepare this for publication, the 2022 Russian invasion of Ukraine is entering its third month. No one knows how this will end. For the first time in their lives, my children and grandchildren are experiencing—along with me—that too-familiar sense of dread that permeated my own younger years. The words of the 1960s protest song come back to haunt: "When will we ever learn?"

The opening segment of this essay was aired on CBC radio's The Sunday Edition *in October, 2012, the fiftieth anniversary of the Cuban Missile Crisis*

X *IN LOCO PARENTIS*

It is winter, 1965. I am cowering in the corner of a closet, trying not to breathe. That's partly because of the dank odor of dirty clothes heaped at my feet, but mostly because I want to remain invisible. I am sick with fear that they will open the door and push aside the shirts and sweatshirts and damp towels that are serving as a shield.

Voices come from the hallway through the open door.

The deeper one says, "We've had a report of a non-student interloper here in Smith Hall. You all know the rules. I'm here to check your rooms."

A mumble of young male voices follows.

"Okay, sure...you can go in my room...yeah, nobody's in mine."

So, it was Blonde Roger they were after, not me. He was somewhere around, at least he had been the night before. I didn't know much about him, but he visited campus often, was tall and thin, easily spotted with his bleached, spiked hair, and I thought maybe he sold drugs. I couldn't even imagine what would happen if they found me instead of him. Well actually, I could imagine and it wasn't good. I was an interloper of another kind.

Only an hour before, I had walked across campus in moonlight, from the south side where all the women were housed in a row of solid brick dormitories connected by a long, enclosed and windowed loggia, to the north side where all the men lived in similar dorms, also connected, but by an open, arched walkway. They didn't have to be locked in at night; we did—at eleven o'clock, twelve on weekends. Starting around ten-thirty, the loggia was lined with couples engaged in passionate good-nights that ended abruptly when the night watchman jangled his keys as a warning. The last of the overwrought young men tore themselves away and the late-returning women rushed through the doors just as the keys turned in the locks.

Then, and only then, was our virtue deemed secure for another night. Of course, there were some girls who dared to stay out all night, but that was a risky business. Despite an active rumour mill and a variety of predictive formulas, no one really knew on which nights a loud bell would signal that all women must be in their own rooms within fifteen minutes for a random bed check. At that point, the house mothers in each dorm began walking up and down the halls making sure all of us were inside the compound.

We didn't call it a compound, but the word seems to fit.

If a woman was missing during a bed check, she would be called before the Dean of Women and asked to explain herself. An honest explanation was almost certain to have her placed on social probation if not expelled. Even a dishonest one. There were no acceptable reasons for being out all night without prior permission.

But never underestimate the ingenuity inspired by young hormones. Every morning the night watchman returned to unlock the loggia doors at five am, and shortly after that a scattering of women could be seen walking through the silent dark to the dorms on north campus where the men lived and the doors were never locked.

The predawn trek from one side to the other was a daring venture, one which I'd undertaken only once before. It now had me hovering in a closet, fearful for my reputation and of expulsion from college.

The deep voice was approaching Jack's room. Jack sounded altogether too welcoming when he invited the Dean of Men to look around. Obviously, he hadn't found Blonde Roger yet. What if he decided to search Jack's closet?

"I did see him yesterday," Jack was saying. "I think he might be visiting someone on second floor."

When word drifted down from the upper floors that the Dean had left the building with Blonde Roger in tow, I stumbled from the closet, disheveled and trembling. It took several hours for my panic to subside, by which time it was mid-morning and the campus had come to life.

I couldn't be seen leaving a men's dorm, so Jack stood guard at the doorway and signaled me when the way was clear.

Not that the men's dorms were always off limits to women. On special, very occasional Open Dorm Sunday afternoons, men and women were free to visit each other's rooms, their passions kept under wraps by the "Open Door, Three Feet on the Floor" rule. House mothers on both sides of campus patrolled the floors to monitor and, presumably, to count feet.

As I slipped out the door of Smith Hall that Sunday morning, it occurred to me that the best strategy would be to take the five-am walk on an Open Dorm Sunday, then leave innocently with all those three-feet-on-the-floor couples who followed the rules. Or, after the morning's fright, maybe it was time I returned to the safer, goody-two-shoes persona that I had only so recently abandoned

•••

The rules were all part of the mindset, entrenched in policy, of *in loco parentis*. Colleges, especially small, co-ed liberal arts colleges like Grinnell, considered it their duty to act on behalf of parents dedicated to protecting their daughters from—well—mostly from boys but also from drugs, booze, and generally inappropriate behaviour. Maybe they were committed to protecting the boys as well, but the boys weren't the ones being locked up and counted. *In loco parentis* protected students from themselves and each other all over the United States until the mid-1960s, when the courts determined that it was in violation of the rights of people who were, in fact, young adults.

In February, 2017, *Psychology Today* ran an article entitled "Controlling the Conduct of College Women in the 1960s." Its author points out that the image of 1960s campuses overrun with "long-haired antiwar protestors, wannabe hippies having promiscuous sex, leftist professors leading 'teach-ins,' and drug fueled rock concerts" does not apply until the late 1960s or 1970s. Indeed, in the early and mid-sixties, keeping track of coeds was paramount, and most colleges had rules similar to, or even more restrictive than the ones I encountered at Grinnell. Just a few years later, all that changed. Dormitories became co-ed, the loggia remained open all night, and bed checks became part of ancient co-ed lore. Perhaps virtue did too, but that was bound to be a losing battle.

Although the possibility of sexual adventure struck the greatest fear in the hearts of the *loco parentis* folks, their concern for our well-being didn't stop there. The list of verboten behaviours included wearing slacks to class or the dining hall, entertaining visitors to campus without advance permission, drinking alcohol, and fraternizing with townies. To enforce these rules, each dorm had a house mother in residence, an elderly single woman living what must have been a lonely life as the guardian of decorum among young women on the cusp of adulthood during the rebellious sixties. There were house mothers in the men's dorms too. I'm not sure what they did. I don't remember anyone feeling anything but mocking disdain for these poor women as they sat at their special table in the dining room or summoned wayward students to their living quarters, just off the lounge where they could easily monitor comings and goings.

I was summoned just once, in the winter of my freshman year, long before the closet episode. I had decided to visit my high school friend, Kathryn, who attended another small college a four-hour bus ride away. I don't remember the circumstances, but I felt an urgent need to get away. Perhaps it had to do with being dumped by my first-ever steady boyfriend over the holidays. I phoned Kathryn, who would be only too happy to see me. She was feeling low, too. We would commiserate together.

According to the rules, I could only sign out to visit a student in another college if I had an invitation from that student's house mother. But this decision was spur-of-the-moment. I didn't have time for that. This was decades before the advent of email.

No problem. My roommate had become quite adept at forging various IDs, and together we wrote a convincing invitation, signed with an elderly scrawl under an imaginary name. I presented it to my housemother and signed out for three days, which I spent hanging out with my friend on a campus not unlike my own—also governed by *in loco parentis*.

When Kathryn's house mother called the two of us into her office, I knew the jig was up.

"You are visiting us from Grinnell, is that right?"

I nodded.

"I know that Grinnell has an invitation requirement, and I don't recall writing an invitation." She turned to my friend. "Kathryn, did you approach me for one?"

Kathryn was mute as well. She shook her head.

"So, Paula, how did you manage this?"

I was not an accomplished liar or breaker-of-rules. I couldn't yet imagine the young woman in the closet. But I knew admitting to forgery was probably not a good idea.

"It was short notice. So I just came," I said. "And I'm leaving this afternoon."

She looked at me sternly over her dark-rimmed glasses. "See that you do."

Why did it surprise me to find a message from my own house mother when I got back to Grinnell? "Please see me when you return." These *in loco* women stayed in touch. Before the inevitable encounter, I had time to sift through my options at leisure, but there really was no way to weasel out of it. She had the evidence in hand. A heavy and unfamiliar dread had settled somewhere between my shoulders and my waist, and I knew the only way to lessen it was to own up. Like finally giving in to nausea by allowing your stomach to empty. I'd rather have vomited.

Oddly, I don't remember the consequences of this transgression, so they can't have been severe. Perhaps those guardians of decorum had softer hearts than we gave them credit for.

A few years ago I visited Grinnell for the first time since I left in 1966. It was winter break; there were no students in sight, but the loggia on South Campus was open. I walked the length of it alone, shivering in the January cold, remembering the steamy evening goodbyes and the race down the length to reach the dining hall at one end before the doors closed. I stopped at the three dorms I had lived in during my three years as a student at Grinnell and wished they were open so I could wander through Cleveland basement, or second floor Loose Hall—presumably named after Somebody-or-Other Loose. I don't remember the name giving rise to gales of laughter and jokes about the women who lived there, but surely it did.

• • •

When, some months after the closet episode, Jack and I decided to get married, I faced the *in loco parentis* mentality one more time. He had been accepted to graduate school at Western Michigan

University in Kalamazoo, which was also home to another small, liberal arts institution, Kalamazoo College. I had one year left before graduation. I'd been on the Dean's List at Grinnell, so I assumed that transferring my credits and graduating from K-College, as it was affectionately called, was a reasonable option. Apparently not. The *in locos* at K-College were in the business of protecting their student body from infiltration by married persons. My academic credentials were stellar, they assured me. But their policy was clear: No off-campus living, so no married students.

Of course. Think about it. What is the principal component of "married bliss" among the young?

After renting an apartment and registering to complete my bachelor's degree at Western Michigan University, a larger institution where many students lived off-campus and where virtue was a hit-or-miss thing, we drove to Pennsylvania for our wedding. There, the age of majority was twenty-one; I was twenty. My parents—not *in loco* this time, but the real thing—had to sign their permission for me to marry.

XI ON BECOMING CANADIAN

In an upstairs apartment in Kalamazoo, Michigan, on June 6, 1968, I was jolted awake by the clock radio. It wasn't the usual morning diet of music and chatter. Sober voices repeated the news for Americans who hadn't stayed up for the late night broadcasts; Bobby Kennedy was dead. Assassinated at midnight, just two months and two days after the assassination of Martin Luther King. Less than five years after the assassination of his brother, JFK. Just five months after the Mai Lai Massacre.

This was my country.

I kicked Jack awake in the bed beside me. Groggily, he sat up and listened. Our eyes met in shared horror and resignation. It was becoming easier and easier to contemplate the big move. In two months we were leaving. Perhaps for good.

We made the decision to move to Canada in the swirling vortex that was 1968. Not only were we disenchanted with our country, we lived in fear of the draft. Jack was in graduate school, but student exemptions were being withdrawn. I was just pregnant—how many children born in the late sixties were conceived in a desperate attempt to keep their fathers safe?—but even parental exemptions were being re-considered as the country scrambled to find young men to fight and die in southeast Asia.

And Canada was only a few hours away.

•••

We drove east from Kalamazoo and reached the Canadian border at Windsor sometime in the afternoon of August 4. I was driving our MGB. Jack was driving a school bus destined to become a camper. It wasn't yet painted in psychedelic colours; that would come later. It was still just an old yellow school bus, filled with all our worldly possessions—a mid 20th century covered wagon with a temperamental transmission, carrying us to the promised land.

Jack had been accepted to graduate school at McMaster University in Hamilton, Ontario. On an earlier two-day trip to check out the city, we had rented an apartment in nearby Dundas. Those two pieces of information were all we had to present to the Canadian immigration officials as we stood confidently before them, two 20-something wanna-be hippies, trying to look respectable, requesting permanent immigrant status. Their response stunned us. We hadn't followed the rules.

There were rules?

It seemed there were, and since we hadn't followed them, permanent resident status was out of the question. Absolutely.

Several hours later, we were continuing east toward Hamilton with a temporary student visa in hand and an uneasy feeling that perhaps changing countries was going to involve some annoying red tape. Who'd have thought? Weren't we the righteous, fleeing the wicked?

We settled quickly into our apartment, and within days we felt like Canadians. Of course there were some small adjustments to make. The coloured money took some getting used to, and we had to work on a few habits of speech—dropping the article before "hospital" and "university", as in "she's in hospital"; referring to French fries as "chips" and dousing them with vinegar; asking for serviettes instead of napkins. The famous Canadian "eh" came quickly and naturally, and I immediately fell in love with CBC radio. In fact, the transition felt almost seamless. Odd, then, that everyone seemed to know we were Americans.

Of course, everyone knew we were Americans. We walked too fast, overtaking real Canadians on the sidewalk. We crossed against the light if no one was coming while real Canadians waited patiently for it to turn green. We displayed our political and social views loudly and unapologetically, while real Canadians spoke gently to avoid offense. We didn't apologize nearly often enough.

The deeply ingrained sense of individualism, entitlement, and righteousness that springs from American history—and that, I suspect, lies deep in the psyche of Americans (and ex-Americans) of all political persuasions—runs counter to equally ingrained Canadian characteristics of compromise, civility, and smugness. I'm not taking sides here; smugness and righteousness are not so different and can be equally tiresome.

• • •

I became a Canadian citizen—yes, after some annoying red tape—in 1975. But I don't know when I shed my American identity. Or if I ever have, entirely. It's easy to change citizenship; you drive across an imaginary line, wait awhile, and swear allegiance to a new nation (and, in this case, a foreign Queen). It's harder to blend in, to truly assimilate, a concept that has become politically incorrect in an increasingly multicultural Canada, where hyphenated citizenship is now the norm and newcomers are often encouraged to maintain two identities.

But not me. I wanted to become as Canadian as I could as quickly as I could. I was in my twenties; I still saw the world as black and white, and I'd fled a country I despised at the time. I quickly assumed an exterior veneer of Canadianism, sang Stompin' Tom Connor songs under my breath, tried to care about hockey, and wrapped myself in the Maple Leaf—not realizing how very un-Canadian a thing that was to do. (Although it is very Canadian to wrap oneself in a flag proclaiming that Canadians do not wrap themselves in flags. This is a distinction foreigners and newcomers can be forgiven for misunderstanding.)

As the years passed, I made the language quirks, the political and social environment, even many Canadian psychological and behavioural tendencies, my own.

I have a friend who grew up with me in central Pennsylvania and has lived as many adult years in North Carolina as I have in Ontario. She noted early on that I had quickly adopted Canadian speech patterns, while she had (and still has) no sign of a North Carolina drawl. When she mentioned this to a colleague of hers, a linguist, he replied, "Your friend in Canada wants to be Canadian. You don't want to be a southerner."

I have now lived in Canada for more than three-quarters of my life, and I'm as Canadian as I'll ever be. During these fifty-plus years, my attitude toward the United States has undergone subtle shifts as both that country and this one have stumbled through the late twentieth and early twenty-first centuries. Those shifts make me no less Canadian. Indeed, ambivalence toward its neighbor to the south is a persistent defining characteristic of Canada. Whatever Canadians are—and this is a subject of endless debate—they're not Americans.

And yet, at some level, I know I am still an American. This realization surfaces at unexpected moments and leaves me realizing that I will always be a hyphenated-Canadian, though I have largely buried that hyphen beneath decades of a growing commitment to my adopted country. I still speak my mind more quickly and more adamantly than most of my friends, but as a Canadian, I apologize for it more now. I am still sometimes caught out by my accent, though I have no idea what subtle American linguistic signals I continue to send. When I return to the rolling and lush mountains of central Pennsylvania, I am filled with a sense of homecoming, and when we visit Jack's family in Connecticut and Massachusetts, I remember the city on the hill. *My country tis of thee*. In these days of apparent American decline, I mourn that distant beacon of freedom and hope along with many Americans.

• • •

A few years ago, CBC radio ran a series called "Twenty Pieces of Music that Changed the World." Number three on the list was "We Shall Overcome." I listened to the analysis of that simple, familiar protest song—its origins, its symbolic impact, the structure of the song itself which begins as a public proclamation and turns deeply inward as a personal commitment—and tears ran down my cheeks. I sang along and was transported to an earlier time and place, arms crossed in front of me, clasping the hands of those beside me, swaying to the steady rhythm of the music, and I felt a pride in my generation of Americans who had not only sung that song but had, in some important ways, overcome—something we are inclined to forget in these days of renewed and growing awareness of inequality and injustice.

The next day, I attended a barbeque with neighbours, all Canadians, and I found myself describing my response to that broadcast to a man of roughly my age.

"Oh yes," said the man, "It was the same here in Canada. I know what you mean."

Well, no, I thought, bristling a bit. It wasn't the same. You cannot feel as I do about the turmoil that was the incubator of my adulthood. Canada has its own shameful past and generational triumphs, but the civil rights movement is not yours.

Neither is the Vietnam War. Years ago I found myself in conversation with a group of friends about that war. These liberal Canadian women held the same views I held about that historical period and were proud of the role Canada had played in welcoming draft dodgers. But as I listened, I realized how relatively untouched they were. If this had been a group of American women of the same age, every one of us would have had a story about how that war had changed the trajectory of our lives or the lives of people we loved. A lost cousin, a paraplegic neighbour, an abandoned education, a life of re-lived trauma. In my case, the happiest of outcomes: an adopted country I have come to love.

• • •

In 1999, I took a part-time teaching job at a Michigan university, an easy commute from my home near the border. I discovered, to my surprise, that I continued to hold American citizenship. I didn't ask for it, didn't want it, but it had followed me silently for three decades. As a result, I didn't need a work visa; but I did need to explain my citizenship status every time I crossed into the U.S.

"Reason for entering the U.S.?"

"Going to work."

"I'll need to see your work visa."

"I'm a naturalized Canadian citizen born in the United States."

"So, you're an American citizen."

"I guess so." Reluctantly, I wanted to say. A residual American citizen. But I'd learned not to be flippant. I needed to get across.

"This is a Canadian passport."

"Yes, I know." I tried not to roll my eyes. *What was your first clue?*

"Why don't you get an American passport?" Silence. Slight shrug.

I couldn't tell this man in the blue uniform with the stars and stripes on his lapel that it's because I no longer feel American. That a decision made thirty years earlier in the heat of a political moment turned out to be irrevocable. That an accident of birth carries less weight than the tangled experiences and commitments of an adult life. That—though I'm often disenchanted with my adopted country—it is my country now. That citizenship means more to me now than it did when I was twenty.

"This one works for me," I said.

They always let me through.

Nearly fifty years after gaining that Canadian passport, I am in the process of formally renouncing my American citizenship. I'd have done it years ago, except that, in order to do so, you have to file income taxes for five consecutive years—something I had not done since moving to Canada in 1968 and was reluctant to begin. An interesting side note: The United States—alone in the world except for Eritrea—taxes based on citizenship rather than residence. Eventually, I chose to face the legal reality. (The financial reality is insignificant, given complex tax treaties between the two countries.) I have now filed for five years and await my turn in line to appear before a consular official to renounce—and pay a whopping renunciation fee. Another uniquely American practice.

You may well ask, why now? Why invest this time and money at my age to alter a status I've had all my life? I ask myself as well. The answer is complex, and not entirely clear even to me. Of course, nobody wants to have a forced relationship with the IRS. But it's more than that.

Recently a friend challenged my decision by declaring national citizenship to be irrelevant, that we are all "citizens of the world". Well, yes. But in this world, we also inhabit a national entity. Decades ago, I consciously chose a country, one that I have come to love, even as I have come to understand its present flaws and historical shames. I have no interest in erasing my past, but I feel no such allegiance to the behemoth south of the border.

XII HOMEMAKING SQUARED

It was a fall day in 1962. My friend and I were walking home from school, kicking dry leaves with our penny-loafered feet, hugging our American history books to our chests.

"I'll go to college, of course," I said. "And have a career. But I do want to get married. Have kids. I really want to be in love."

She nodded in agreement. We all wanted to be in love.

"I don't like housework, though," I said.

She thought a minute. "Well, maybe it's different when you're doing it for someone you love."

•••

On a hot June afternoon in 1980, I stretch my back and look up at the hills and fields, barely taking in the view. I've been picking peas for fifteen minutes now, and already have a full pail with two more rows to go. Before the kids get home from school, I should have them shelled and frozen in bags. Then, I'll have to clean up the kitchen mess and figure out supper before Jack gets home. Here's hoping the cows don't break through the fence again today and scuttle my grand plans.

The first peas out of the pods make a ping-sound as they hit the bottom of the pan. It takes forever until enough cover the bottom to lower the tone to a tiny thud. The mess on the counter mocks me from the other side of the kitchen.

If housework was different when doing it for someone you loved, something was missing in this equation. First of all, the person I loved didn't care much about housework, so it was never clear I was doing it for him. I liked to think he might notice if it never got done, but I wasn't sure.

The pan of shelled peas was slowly filling. How had I come to think I'd found my place in the world, growing and freezing vegetables? Worrying about cows breaking through fences?

I was sure I'd have ended up somewhere far more impressive, but for some hastily-made decisions on the cusp of adulthood. Like marrying a guy who was smart as a whip but had no interest in social status. Like buying a farm in northern Ontario because I'd read a book on organic foods and well, you know, one thing led to another. Like looking at my baby daughter and saying to the job market, "Not yet. I can't leave yet." And saying it again looking at a second baby, and then again looking at a third, until one day I realized I already had a job. I didn't have an office or a very impressive resume, but I was pretty sure I had tenure.

Now would be the time to describe how I came to love the idyllic life of a country wife and mom—notwithstanding the kitchen counter and the pea-shelling—and assure you that I never looked back. But that would be a lie. I did often love it, but I looked back all the time. I stared at half-cleared paths toward un-reached destinations: the halls of academe, the front lines of social action, the Booker short list. I squirmed with a sense of inadequacy as more and more of my school friends reached such destinations.

But not me. In the era of Betty Friedan and Germaine Greer, I was a homemaker. More than a homemaker. Or less. A farmwife.

Homemaker. One who manages a home. Especially one who is a spouse and parent.
Farmwife. A farmer's wife.
(I was also a professor's wife, but that's not in the dictionary. The professor and the farmer are the same guy.)

Like the good manager she was, my own mom had made her job seem effortless most of the time. And—unlike the slaves to the patriarchy depicted in *The Feminine Mystique*—Mom seemed content. She had a rich life filled with friends and volunteer commitments outside the home. Sometimes, she read a book instead of doing the dishes. But she never forgot her main job: food always appeared on the table, clean sheets tucked in with hospital corners appeared on the beds, socks were neatly sorted into pairs.

Without a word of thanks, I took my well-managed self out into the vortex of the 1960s where I quickly dismissed Mom's role, if not her very self, as inconsequential. I would not fall into the homemaker trap. I would become liberated from the drudgery of vacuum cleaners and pot roasts. I would be busy building a new world order.

Drudgery. Dull, irksome, and fatiguing work; uninspiring or menial labour.

•••

It is 1968, and I am pregnant with my first child. The pregnancy is actually part of the plan for a new world order, and I am quite excited about it, in a liberated kind of way. I realize I am young—only twenty-three—and this is not exactly how I'd imagined life unfolding, but I am keeping my equally young husband out of the clutches of his draft board. So succumbing to my un-liberated longing for a child has become a political act, and therefore acceptable.

And I have a plan. I will finish my Master's Degree a few months before the baby is born. Then, I'll stay home with it for a few months. I'll breast-feed, because that's best for the baby, but just for a few months because otherwise I'll be tied down. Then I'll start looking for a job. In the meantime, we have moved to Canada because the draft board changed its rules for exemption and the baby has now become one of many futile political acts of the era.

"I think I'll put the baby in daycare after a few months," I tell my mom, who is visiting us in our basement apartment in Dundas, Ontario. "I'd like to get a job, do something meaningful with my life."

She looks at me strangely and answers tentatively, even defensively. "If you go to work, Paula, you will have to accept the fact that—to a large extent—someone else will be raising your child."

I don't think she really gets it. Should I succumb to the drudgery of homemaking, or should I become a person of worth? What kind of choice is that?

I don't think Mom's read Betty Friedan.

The baby is adorable. A roly-poly blond baby girl. And it turns out it's not going to be that easy getting a job in Canada with no job experience and a Master's Degree in American History. So my plan isn't working out so well. I've met a couple of other grad student wives with babies who've decided to stay home with them. I've become good friends with one of them whose baby boy is named Che, after Che Guevara. Obviously, she's liberated. Her blond hair is very long, and she wears bell-bottomed jeans with flowers embroidered on them. She also talks a lot about earth-mother kind of stuff, which is, to me, a new way of looking at the whole liberation thing. It makes me think I shouldn't have stopped breast feeding. It really is hard to get it right.

After reading some books about natural food and healthy living, I plant a small garden and begin baking bread and lacing our soup with brewer's yeast. In order to escape drudgery, I join ZPG, an organization committed to Zero Population Growth, and decide that our next baby will be adopted. When he arrives, a ten-day-old bundle, I realize that I have joined the earth-mother brigade. I am in the process of discovering something disconcerting from which I have never fully recovered: There is a fair measure of satisfaction in managing a home.

Satisfaction: a happy or pleased feeling because of something that you did or something that happened to you; the act of providing what is needed or desired.

In time, I struck my own bargain with the homemaker devil. I stayed home with my children to make a home, but to make it worthwhile—to convince myself I was a woman of worth—I reverted to an earlier image of home, one based on the pioneer life of Laura Ingalls Wilder and the dietary imperatives of Adele Davis. It ultimately landed me on a 300-acre farm with goats, chickens, cows, sheep, pigs. Homemaking squared.

By tossing aside my academic credentials, by forging an identity based on homemaking, was I being a traitor to my gender? Should I have followed one of those paths toward a feminist future before they were overgrown with brambles? In truth, I've never stopped wondering.

•••

It is 1972. I am in the living room of a woman I barely know, invited here because—well, in fact, I'm not quite sure why. Because we are both women and this is a Women's Lib meeting, I guess. Because she senses that we share a commitment to feminism. Because I am new in this place and she, kindly, believes this is a way for me to meet like-minded women. I am grateful, but somewhat uncomfortable, as I always am in groups of strangers who appear to know who they are and what they're about.

I have arrived here with another woman I know better, a friend I have made during our first months living on the farm. We two are the rural component in this group of urban women whose feminism has led them to reject the straitjacket into which the prevailing culture has entrapped us. I have rejected that strait-jacket too.

Or, I think I have. By the end of the meeting, cups of tea and friendly chat notwithstanding, I'm no longer sure.

Perhaps it would have been better to remain silent, but that's a straitjacket woven of another fabric, and it's not my style. So I—we, for if anything my friend is more outspoken than I—leap to the defense of women who stay home with children, women who choose to focus on traditional domestic skills, women who are committed to traditional marriage, women who (and this renders us beyond the pale) have decided to apply their energies to living off the land. Retrograde.

It seems we are unworthy spokespersons for our gender, willing victims of patriarchal repression.

I have been here before. Several years earlier, in another city, I attended a demonstration in support of women's rights. I was a newcomer there, too, standing alone on the curbside when a couple of fellow-demonstrators approached me, extending the hand of friendship. We chatted. Yes indeed, like them I supported abortion rights, the rights of lesbians, equal rights and opportunities for all women. And what did I do, they asked. Well, I had a three-month-old baby. I was staying at home with her, while her father finished his PhD. The women's sympathy was overwhelming. Should he not have been at home while I continued my studies? No, I protested. I was thrilled to be staying home with her. It was, indeed, what I wanted to do. The women drifted away leaving me to wonder if I was a disgrace to the sisterhood.

I don't judge them harshly, those earnest women from both cities. Indeed, I am grateful for all they and their cohorts accomplished. It was early days in a movement that matured to be more inclusive. They were as young as I was; all of us too young, it now seems to me, to see past our current passions and circumstances, to imagine what lay beyond. For them, perhaps, the surprising intensity of maternal love, the unexpected satisfaction of the mundane; for me, the societal pressures so well disguised as choice, the uncomfortable fact that you can't change the world without venturing into it.

I was content with my choice much of the time, but in making the larger point I ought not overstate my level of satisfaction. There is drudgery everywhere, and I am no fan. In the house, dishes piled up on the kitchen counter, bread crusts and apple cores piled up under children's beds, dust bunnies multiplied. In a farm kitchen, the muddy footprints crossing the kitchen floor are only partly mud, and sometimes the house smelled like a barn. The mess on the counter often included eggs with hen poop and straw stuck to them and a slimy piece of cheesecloth from straining fresh milk. In the barn, water lines froze and baby goats died. Manure piled up in calf stalls, demanding hours of hard labour. The cow needed to be milked and the animals fed even when the whole family was sick with the flu.

I often railed against the grime, inconvenience, and physically demanding work—the drudgery. Those alternate paths felt hopelessly far away, my own decisions sadly irreversible. And yet there were, in fact, opportunities to reverse them. I didn't know then, and I don't know now, whether I passed them up out of inertia or principle. I do know that there were enough moments of joy—in the house with the children, in the barn with the animals, in the stillness of early mornings—to hold me.

I wasn't content being "just" a housewife—even a farmwife—for long. I was, after all, a product of the sixties. But as I searched for meaningful alternatives, I began to realize that most, like homemaking, involved a balance between satisfaction and drudgery, and that in the grand scheme of things, those years spent at home with children, learning the timeless arts of self-sufficiency and domesticity, and adapting my life to the vagaries of weather and nature, were about as meaningful as it gets.

Housewife: 1) a married woman whose main occupation is caring for her family, managing household affairs, and doing housework.
2) a small container for needles, thread, and other small sewing items.

XIII WHAT AM I BID FOR THIS FINE PIANO?

My most impressive musical accomplishment is Mozart's Piano Sonata in C; except for the part toward the end of the second movement where a bunch of flats insinuate themselves into the music line and trick me every time, I think it sounds pretty good. Most of my repertoire is at a much more elementary level, so I like to keep the book open to that page. That way, if anyone passing by the piano notices all those dense black notes, gasps, and says "You can play that?" I can leap right in and play a few bars. It's a sham. I consider it more fanciful than dishonest.

Of course, in order to have Mozart's Sonata on display, you need to have a piano—something I have always considered an essential piece of household furniture, whether anyone plays or not. So, soon after we bought a house, we bought a piano, an old upright from the classifieds for fifty dollars. It was badly scratched and didn't hold a tune very well, but it was good enough for me. Until the piano at an auction in the summer of 1975 caught my eye.

This wasn't a farm auction. No tractors or pig troughs. It included household goods and antiques, and it was being held at a lakeside resort along the north shore of Lake Huron.

When we showed up, a crowd was already milling around the resort, which had recently been converted to a commune by a group of young people from Toronto. The only item of interest to me was a beautiful old player piano.

Player pianos gained popularity in the late nineteenth and early twentieth centuries, before the days of radios and record players. They were upright pianos with a self-playing option that used pedals to pump air through holes in a roll of perforated paper. The force of the air pressed keys to play whatever music had been programmed into the roll—from The Beer-Barrel Polka to Beethoven. I remembered, as a child, pumping the pedals of a neighbour's player piano and watching the keys move up and down as if by magic. This would allow me to carry my propensity for musical deception to a whole new level!

"A beautiful old player piano in perfect working order..." crooned the auctioneer. At two hundred, Jack reminded me in a stage whisper that we already had a piano that I almost never played. I ignored him. But at three-fifty, I shook my head, and Jack let go a relieved sigh.

We were almost back to the car when one of the commune members — a tall, slim man with long hair, in jeans, a purple tie-dyed shirt, and leather sandals—came running up. He introduced himself as Luke.

"If you're still interested in that piano, it turns out the other guy doesn't want it after all. So you can have it for your highest bid." Jack gave me a defeated look. Luke continued, "I hate to be without a piano, but we really need the dough. We want to start homesteading, you know, buy goats and all."

We did know. Our own attempts at self-sufficiency were undergoing revision as we moved away from our homesteading image—with goats—to a full-fledged farm.

Jack looked thoughtful, then spoke. "In fact, we have several goats we'd like to sell. We also have a piano, not great, but decent. We'll give you our piano, two milking goats, and a female kid in exchange for the player piano."

"Thanks for checking with me," I muttered. But I couldn't really disagree. We had already decided it was time for the goats to go. We couldn't manage to keep them fenced in, and they had already destroyed our only apple tree. We had a small herd of cows, including one milk cow. The goats had become superfluous.

That evening, after Luke and a helper unloaded our new piano, carried it into the living room, and strapped our old one upright in the back of his truck, I brought the goats from the barn. "Good girls," I said, stroking their backs. They looked at me with their doleful, intelligent eyes. Erowyn, Gloin, Pippin. These goats had been with us for the birth of this dream—had helped deliver it, in fact—and were now moving on to fuel someone else's while we built a herd of mostly-nameless cows. I couldn't control the tears as the two men loaded them into the passenger space of the club-cab pickup truck.

When they were out of sight, I wiped tears from my eyes and peered into the cardboard box Luke had left with the piano—leather bellows, dozens of small leather fittings, and a stack of narrow, oblong boxes of music rolls.

The next morning, I called our piano tuner.

Mr. Fleming emerged from his blue panel van—coughing into a handkerchief with one hand and carrying his worn leather satchel in the other—and slowly wheezed his way to the back door. I was always relieved, when he drove away, that he hadn't expired on my living room floor. It would happen in someone's house, I was sure.

Once inside, he put down his bag and rested a moment on the round piano stool. Then, rasping and coughing, he began aligning all the sound waves with a variety of tuning forks, up and down the keyboard, tightening one string after another as he went.

Finally, he sat on the stool, tested a few chords, and began to play. He played Bach, blues and ragtime. His face, framed by sparse, fly-away white hair, relaxed into a contented smile

When he was finished, he said, "These old player uprights were well made. Even without the player parts, you've got yourself a good piano here."

"I do have the player parts," I said, placing the box of bellows and leather fittings on the floor beside him.

He pulled out the bellows, turned them over in his hands, and shook his head. "You can't use these," he said. "The leather's shot. They'll never hold air. It'd cost more to repair these parts than the piano is worth."

"Call me in the fall, after you've started heating," he said as he left. "It'll need a re-tuning then."

I hoped he'd still be alive in the fall.

In fact, Mr. Fleming continued wheezing and tuning pianos for years. When he retired, the new piano tuner came with his electronic gadgets, tuned the piano in half the time, charged twice the price, and left without playing a concert. On the other hand, I was pretty sure he wouldn't die on me.

That afternoon, I phoned Luke, prepared to do battle.

"This piano is not what we were promised. The player function doesn't work and can't be fixed. You'll have to return the two milking goats. You can keep the kid. She's pure Nubian and worth quite a lot. Or, you can pay us 100 dollars and keep them all."

Luke was having none of it.

"That piano is fine. You need to find a player piano specialist who knows what he's doing. I'll give you the name of someone in Toronto."

Toronto. That would be 700 kilometers away.

"This may not be Toronto, Luke, but I'm not stupid. I can see the holes in the leather. Is that why the first bidder backed out?"

Luke was silent. Then, "I'm sorry. A deal is a deal."

And we're suckers, I thought.

When I told the whole story to my friend Edith the next day, she said "Let's go get 'em." On the way, in her van, we rehearsed the kidnapping plan.

While I went searching for Luke, Edith—rope in hand—took charge of the rescue operation. When I saw the goats tethered to a post with almost nothing to eat, any qualms I had about this adventure evaporated. By the time I found Luke in his cabin, leaning back on the bed, smoking a joint, Edith had Gloin and Erowyn in the van. I hated leaving Pippin behind.

It took Luke a moment to recognize me.

"I've come for the goats. I'm taking the two does. Make sure the kid gets enough to eat."

He stared at me blankly, then said, "Perhaps someday you will learn that there are honest people in the world, Paula."

He stood up and closed the cabin door on me.

I know those were his words. I remember them clearly. And although it sounded straightforward enough, I'm not really sure what he meant to say. Maybe he was stoned and didn't know, himself. I suppose he thought he was being honest, though I still think the facts speak for themselves. Certainly I thought I was being honest, though in fact I suspect that our new piano—even without the player parts—was worth more than we ended up paying for it in goods and goats. It was, as Mr. Fleming said, a good piano.

Whatever its symbolic value as a measure of personal honesty, that piano enjoyed a place of prominence in our home for years. I continued to play sporadically and badly: the Music Box Dancer was a favourite then, and I worked on some Bach Two-part Inventions that I'd partially mastered as a teenager. But I returned again and again to the Mozart Sonata, the one that looked so good on the page, the piece most likely to impress.

XIV BUTTER WITH THAT?

My decision to devote my life to raising children and helping to run a family farm never went more than a few months without triggering an identity crisis. As a younger woman, I had imagined myself an outstanding scholar or an ambassador for world peace. Seriously. My life goal at the age of sixteen—at which point most adolescents are beginning to confront reality—was to be the U.S. Ambassador to the United Nations. This was before high school guidance offices were equipped with interactive life-planning software to help students align their goals with market realities. Of course, now that I had married and moved to Canada, the U.S. authorities would have had trouble finding my phone number. Canada had an ambassador to the U.N. too, but the Canadians hadn't yet discovered me, and I feared they never would, stuck as I was changing diapers, milking cows, and shovelling manure.

By my mid-thirties, I knew the ambassador thing was out. But still, I felt I had something to offer beyond the confines of the home and farm. My youngest child's arrival five years earlier had allowed me to linger in my homemaking-farming role a bit longer—more comfortable there than I thought I should be—but as he climbed onto the school bus that September, I realized the time had come to move on. Jack brought in a good teaching salary, but the farm—well, the farm consumed as much cash as it generated.

I didn't want to stop parenting and farming. Not at all. I was looking for a part-time add-on that would allow me to add "professional woman" to my resume and contribute to the family income. In that order of priority.

I did a lot of soul-searching between trips to the barn and driving kids to music lessons. Should I return to university for a Ph.D. or some saleable qualification? Teacher? Counsellor? Librarian? All the options for further education meant leaving Jack, the kids, and the farm for an extended period. I knew my reluctance to do that deprived the world of a great talent, but I just couldn't. Sorry, world. Maybe later. I considered writing; I'd always thought of myself as a writer-in-waiting. I pulled out my old typewriter and banged out some paragraphs about the farm, about Lake Superior—a dozen or so maudlin, cliché-ridden pages before concluding I hadn't waited long enough.

I followed up a few possibilities from the local classifieds, but wasn't interested in a job in retail or as a receptionist.

"Illusions of grandeur," scoffed my friend Anna. "Do you want a job or not?"

Easy for her. She had been a teacher, could return to being a teacher whenever she wanted. I was a…well…nothing. A housewife and a farmer in northern Ontario with a master's degree in American history. Not much more in demand than a UN Ambassador.

Given my illusions of grandeur and a deeply held aversion to all things commercial, it may strike you as strange that I looked twice at the advertisement for a muffin franchisee. Actually, Jack saw the ad first, which I figure makes him the fall guy in this story. I'm sure he knows I blamed him for all that followed, though I never accused him directly.

And it did have its appeal. By borrowing money against the farm, I could become a business owner—a bit less cerebral than the professional life I'd envisioned for myself, but the wholesome image of freshly baked muffins complemented my back-to-the-land persona, and the prospects for profit went some way to satisfy my illusions of grandeur, though I would have preferred selling books or stationery supplies. But my options were limited. I decided it was time to work on my visceral disdain for the world of business and leap into muffins.

There didn't seem to be much of an application process for acquiring the franchise aside from filling out a few forms and signing on the dotted line, first with the bank and then with the head office. I showed up for my first day of training at the franchise's flagship operation in Toronto's Union Station, where I was immediately wrapped in an apron and put in the hands of the head baker. It was instantly clear to me that this would be much messier—or differently messy—than international diplomacy. By the end of my week's training, I knew how to prepare basic white and bran muffin mixes in humungous tubs, exactly how many nuts, raisins, or chocolate chips to add, how to use an ice cream scoop to fill muffin tins with batter, how to wipe the tins clean after baking, how to make coffee, use a cash register, wear a hair net, fill out a daily muffin report, and take monthly inventory. I was not bubbling with enthusiasm, but surely that would come.

By the time I arrived back in the Sault, the little muffin kiosk in the mall was taking shape. I had to be on hand to accept deliveries of corn oil, flour, sugar, and other dry ingredients; eggs and buttermilk would arrive the day before opening. With one week to go, I established myself at a table in the mall food court and began interviewing potential employees: two full-time bakers and four part-time counter people.

Here's how it would work: The morning baker would arrive very early, mix batter and get muffins in the ovens. Counter staff would arrive at opening time. I would saunter in mid-morning after milking the cow, collecting the eggs, putting the children on the school bus, and tidying up the house. Maybe I'd play the piano a bit if I had time. Once on site I would help out at the counter when it was busy, order supplies, check the previous day's cash and muffin reports, and arrive back home in time to meet the school bus and get supper ready. I'd have a half-time job and get fabulously rich.

Three days before opening, the huge yellow and blue sign went up over the curved plexiglass counter: *mmmarvellous mmmuffins*. The same day, Gino—a small, wiry guy who oozed something that I'm sure he thought was charm—arrived from the head office to assist with the opening.

Gino tried his best to teach me the basics of marketing. I was a reluctant student. When the local newspaper arrived to interview me about this new enterprise, Gino stepped in and lied about the number of employees. Ten, he said. I tried to correct him. I scolded him when the interviewer left. Seven, not ten. And mostly part time.

He scolded me back. "You have to make it sound more impressive. That's how business works."

When muffins didn't fly out at the rate we'd expected for opening day, Gino decided the problem was that nobody had noticed us. Nobody had noticed the huge blue and yellow sign. Nobody had noticed the aroma of freshly-baked muffins. Nobody had noticed the smiling sales girl in her blue and white baker's hat. We had to do something to draw attention to the place.

"Maybe they just don't want muffins," I said.

He looked at me as though I'd lost my last marble.

"We'll get their attention," he said and wandered into the middle of the mall where he pretended to stumble against a garbage container opposite the shop. It fell with a crash, causing mall patrons to pause in place and me to cringe behind the cash register (or, as Gino called it to my horror, the "Jewish piana"). What had I got myself into? People were noticing Gino and the garbage can. I hoped they weren't noticing me. In any case, they weren't rushing to buy muffins.

"Opening days are a huge success in the cities," said Gino, leaving the upended garbage can for mall staff to deal with. "Maybe people in this little place just aren't sophisticated enough for muffins. Maybe it's more a donut kind of town."

By the end of the first week, I already knew: I really didn't care if people ate muffins. In fact, when—rarely—customers crowded around the counter, I became claustrophobic and annoyed. I wanted to shout, "Shoo! Go! Buy a donut! Buy a waffle!" Instead, I forced a smile and said "Butter with that?"

But maybe it would grow on me. In the meantime, I resigned myself to a week or two of long days to get things running smoothly before I could settle into my half-day, arm's length, professional woman routine.

Now, those of you reading this who have some experience with business are no doubt saying smugly to yourselves, "Ha. Silly woman. That'll never work. She's going to have to jump right into the batter up to her armpits all day long." Well, you'd be wrong. You would have underestimated the strength of my commitment to have it all. The kids, the home, the farm, and the job.

It took a couple of months, not a couple of weeks, but I did turn *mmmuffins* into a half-time job. That is, if you don't count the income side of that equation. Occasionally I was able to write myself a cheque, but it didn't add up to minimum wage for even the several hours a day I spent there. Partly because, within a few months of opening in the fall of 1980, Canada fell into a deep recession. Partly because I chose to pay others so I could continue with the parts of my life I really cared about. Mostly because I didn't have the know-how or the commitment to promote and grow the business. While other *mmmarvelous mmmuffins* franchises in Canada turned tidy profits, even during the recession, mine barely managed to pay the monthly franchise fees.

Every day, at mall closing time, the baker packed up the leftovers and set them aside for me to pick up the next day. It was an iron-clad franchise rule: we could not sell day-olds. Ever. On good days, there weren't many left-overs. On bad days, dozens. I had a surreptitious underground business delivering day-olds to friends. (Oh, right. There I go again, forgetting that commerce involves exchanges of cash for goods. Okay. Correction. I gave a lot of day-olds away.) But it didn't take long for my family and everyone I knew to grimace at the sight of yet another over-sized muffin. Even the chocolate fudge, the least muffinesque of all, ceased to appeal. I could sometimes pass them off in a trifle or cut them into finger-sized pieces to serve with tea or coffee. Occasionally we delivered leftovers to nursing homes, though even that was technically against franchise rules.

Here's where we happened upon a happy marriage between the farm and the muffin business: chocolate-chip-muffin-fed pork. Bran-muffin fortified eggs. The most lucrative aspect of the muffin business showed up on the farm's balance sheet, in the column labelled animal feed.

Of course, head office noticed that their monthly franchise fee was pretty puny, so they kept sending Gino to find out what was wrong. The more he pressured me to become more aggressive about marketing, the more sullen I became about the whole enterprise.

"I'd rather die than take advice from that weasel," I said to anyone who would listen. But he persisted.

"A muffinwich?? What the hell is a muffinwich?" I asked when he decided in year two that my store would be the trial site for a new product: a bran muffin shaped like a hamburger bun filled with tuna salad. Or egg salad. Your choice. Or not. Not, it quickly became clear. The muffinwich had no impact on my bottom line, and no other franchise ever introduced the product.

After the longest four years of my life, I sold the business for enough to pay off the bank. Jack, who had been good-natured throughout, shrugged in resignation. "It's no worse than if you'd bought a brand new Cadillac, not bothered to insure it, and driven it into the river," he said.

Well, not to put too fine a point on it, whose idea was it, anyway?

Fact is, if Jack's imaginary Cadillac accident had happened, I'd have been burdened by guilt. Or drowned. When mmmuffins finally left my life, I felt giddy and light. I had been the world's worst businessperson, and I'd escaped debt free and a wee bit wiser.

The only ones who really missed the muffin business were the pigs.

XV PUTTING UP SIGNS AND HOPING FOR THE BEST

"It's the right thing to do," said Pappy.

"That's not how Mae and Warren see it." Grammy took a sip of coffee and looked through the door into the living room, where my parents hovered near the radio.

It was June 19, 1953 and we were visiting my grandparents—the fun ones—though no one seemed to be having fun just then. They were alert to something happening far away. I watched them tensing, listening, shaking their heads in dismay.

"If they're traitors, they should die. That's it," said Pappy.

"They" were Julius and Ethel Rosenberg, convicted spies for the Soviet Union, sentenced to death in New York's Sing Sing Prison. A last-minute stay of execution had delayed their electrocution, but it was overturned a day later. When the word came that the sentence had been carried out, my parents turned off the radio.

"What happened?" I asked.

Dad tried to explain so that an eight-year-old could understand.

"Two people have been put to death in an electric chair."

"Why? Did they do something really bad?"

"Maybe," said Dad. "But their trial wasn't fair. And killing people never makes things better."

These were the early years of the Cold War, the McCarthy era in the United States, the years when I first became aware of the world beyond the walls of my comfortable home. This is my second memory of political awareness, the first being the taunting song about Adlai Stevenson I brought home from first grade.

As my political sensitivities matured, and as the fifties gave way to the sixties, I became an advocate for political activism, certain I would become an effective force for good.

In Civics Class, I spoke out against capital punishment. I cheered on the civil rights demonstrations hundreds of miles to the south. I sang "Where Have All the Flowers Gone" along with long-haired, guitar-playing protesters. As a college student, I ventured a bit further, joining civil rights and anti-war marches in cities near my Midwest college.

Then I got married. Moved to Canada. Had kids. Bought a farm. Adopted a lifestyle focused more on home grown vegetables than on peace and social justice. I still spoke out…but feebly, and my reluctance to offend dampened my voice in the conservative rural valley that had become home.

Somewhere along the line, it dawned on me that advocating political activism is not the same as being a political activist. It's a distinction I've had trouble reconciling all my adult life. I've been quick to voice an opinion, much less willing to take risks associated with that opinion.

Cautious. Or cowardly.

• • •

When I re-gained a fire in my belly, it wasn't to fight war or racism. My young children were coming home from school with stories of their classmates being sent to the office for "the strap"— a punishment I thought had gone out with kerosene lanterns. They also shared stories about the teachings of the "Bible Lady" who came into the school once a week to spread the gospel, which included terrifying old testament tales of God's revenge, and her own interpretations applied to eastern religions. Like everyone in Japan ending up in hell because they worship idols.

I scheduled a visit to the school principal, armed with arguments against corporal punishment and in favour of the separation of church and state. It seemed the use of the strap was sanctioned by the Ontario Education Act (about which I knew nothing). And as for the evangelist: this was Canada, not the United States (where everyone knew I came from). There was—in 1975—no enforced separation of church and state.

"Canada is a Christian country," he said.

I was, of course, free to have my children removed from the classroom during the Bible Lady's visits. They could sit alone in the hall.

I didn't choose to banish them to the hall. Instead, I tried to inoculate them at home with a gentler religious perspective, but I had been energized by a cause. The next year, I ran for and won a seat on the local school board, where I managed to voice my opinions about evangelism and corporal punishment—a voice in the wilderness, as it turned out. But I had found a niche that suited me, and one term followed another until I became—I'm loathe to admit—part of the establishment. Within a few years, the Ontario provincial legislature had banned both the strap and the Bible Lady without any help from me, and I had learned to choose my battles more strategically. Or to compromise my principles. I've never been sure which.

For several years in the early 1990s, I represented northern Ontario on the province-wide association of school boards, eventually serving two years as its president—a position with a modest public profile for those interested in the politics of education. My name appeared in the papers often, speaking on behalf of public school boards; I showed up occasionally on the television news; I was an invited guest to radio and television talk shows.

By the time the Provincial Liberal Party asked me to run for a seat in the provincial legislature in 1995, I had developed a taste for public life. I enjoyed—okay, I revelled in—the sense that I was a fish swimming in bigger and bigger waters, and growing as I moved, like a gold fish that's poured from a child's fishbowl to an aquarium, and then into an outdoor pool. The more space they have, the bigger they grow.

After all, I'd been waiting for someone to discover me all my life. As a child at the ice-skating rink, as a pre-teen at social dance classes, as a fourteen-year-old standing in the arch between the living room and the dining room, singing along to the Everly Brothers, as a young woman going about her daily tasks—always, a talent scout or journalist looked on from the shadows, in search of an undiscovered star or an exemplary human being. At last…I had made the cut.

Hopes were high. The existing government, led by the province's social democratic party, the New Democrats (NDP), was wildly unpopular. The Liberals were leading in the polls when the election was called in May.

•••

"Would you consider putting up a sign?"

These nice folks had invited me in and seemed supportive—a pleasant change from the bored or openly hostile response I was receiving in most quarters.

"Well, sure," said the grey-haired man. "You seem like a nice lady. You can put up a sign. But mind you, we don't vote."

Lots of people don't vote. A discouraging number. But these people had been attentive, asked me questions, seemed like concerned citizens.

"Why not?" I asked.

I knew, of course, that some of the Christian fundamentalists consider political involvement, even voting, to be contrary to the teachings of Christ. Something about rendering unto Caesar. Or not. But then, they wouldn't agree to a sign. So this must be something else.

His wife spoke up. "Oh, we did once," she said. "But it didn't work. You go ahead and put up your sign and we'll hope for the best."

I resisted the temptation to launch into a quick lesson on participatory democracy and civic responsibility. I had a lot of doors to knock on. So I thanked them for their time, urged them to try voting once again, got a hammer and a sign from the trunk of my little red Honda hatchback, and pounded the red-and-white sign into their lawn. I doubt they turned up at the polls.

Neither, I'm sure, did the man who met my campaign volunteer with a rifle and insisted that I was a bitch. No, he'd never met me, knew nothing about me—except, I presume, that I was female. The only good politician anywhere, anytime, was Hitler, he said before slamming the door in my worker's face. Best that he stay home on election day.

Then, there was the guy who took a shine to me because he thought I might be able to get his teeth fixed. I still remember his name, but to respect his privacy, I'll call him Otto. Otto lived alone in a remote, northern corner of the riding, and when he opened the door to his ramshackle home, I had the feeling no one else had knocked on it in a very long time. I got a good, long look at his foul-smelling mouth, full of rotting teeth and red gums, and an even longer harangue about the existing MPP's failure to deal with him. I felt a sudden, profound sympathy for my opponent, and I wondered if this one vote was really worth it, but I made soothing noises about the need to extend provincial health coverage to include dental care—not really part of the party platform—which I guess he took as a commitment to fix his teeth. Every few days, until the campaign ended, Otto phoned my campaign office to profess his undying affection for me and to remind me about his teeth—while I tried to forget the gruesome image of his gaping maw. I have no way of knowing whether he ever made it to a polling station.

Of course, these are the stand-outs. The month-long campaign consisted of day after day of door-knocking, leaflet distributing, occasional public events and debates with the other two candidates, restless nights in uncomfortable hotels scattered throughout the huge north-eastern Ontario riding of Algoma—a rural electoral district twice the size of Massachusetts with a population of less than 50,000 people—and phone-in pep-talks and updates from the party leader before the days of easy electronic communication.

The Canadian parliamentary system demands a partisan solidarity that holds elected members—and candidates—to the party line and encourages a strident response to the opposition. It takes goldfish and turns them into sharks.

That was a problem, because I had never been—still am not—stridently partisan. I was running for the party that I generally support, although I have always teetered on its left edge and have sometimes tumbled into the arms of the NDP. Indeed, were it not for NDP's tendency toward dogmatism, I might have joined their ranks. But I was a Liberal candidate and so—although I had trouble personally objecting to many of the policies of the existing NDP government—my job was to oppose them as vigorously as possible.

I did my best. I followed the party's prepared script—okay, occasionally adding things like provincial dental coverage as I deemed them appropriate. I bashed the economic performance of the outgoing government without understanding much about economics. I assured rural neighbours and the broader constituency that, as a provincial politician, I had no opinion about the new, federally-imposed gun registration though in fact I supported it wholeheartedly. I privately assured my lesbian friend that once elected, I would argue for gay adoption rights, but I publicly supported the party's less forthright position, designed not to offend right-leaning voters. In public debates, I threw darts at the NDP incumbent, a man for whom I had, in fact, considerable respect.

I slept well at night from sheer exhaustion.

God knows, I tried to hone my shark's teeth. But I—and my distressed campaign manager—knew it was a losing battle when, immediately after accosting the incumbent in a debate, I turned and apologized to him.

"Oh, sorry," I said. "Nothing personal."

It's a moment that still haunts me with a combination of embarrassment (for not being a good candidate) and pride (for not being a good candidate).

Clearly, I wasn't a born campaigner. But I was convinced that, once elected, I would be a good parliamentarian. I would display even-handed rational thought; I would eschew dogmatic single-mindedness; I would promote compromise; I would be a model of principled decision-making and do my best to promote civil and responsible government. I would listen to all sides of a debate, even when they challenged my convictions.

In fact, I'd have been eaten alive.

We speak glibly of people having the courage of their convictions as though firm convictions automatically confer bravery. I'm not so sure of that. Are those politicians who refuse to budge more courageous than those who allow their convictions to be challenged? Quite the contrary, I think, but alas, the un-budgeables are more electable at a time when sound-bites and memes trump reasonable argument. And at some point, among all but the strongest, the increasingly rare willingness to be swayed by argument and evidence becomes confused with a willingness to be swayed by the promise of personal gain, the desire for peer support, or the sheer headiness of power. That's where the real courage comes in, and I fear I would not have had it—that I would have rapidly disintegrated from the inside out, becoming co-opted by more dogmatic, partisan colleagues and losing all sense of myself.

I will never know of course, because I suffered a humiliating defeat, as did the Liberal Party, that June. The province elected a mean-spirited Conservative government, which imposed its "Common Sense Revolution" on Ontario for the next eight years.

The reasons for my own defeat were many and complex. My rural, northern riding was probably not ready to elect a woman. I learned later that both the Conservative and NDP candidates celebrated when I was nominated because they knew, no matter how good I might be, I couldn't win. The province-wide surge to the right pulled centrist votes in that direction, leaving me in third place, behind the Conservative. The NDP incumbent won the riding. In fact, he deserved to win; he'd represented the small, widely-scattered communities well for many years.

It took weeks for me to emerge from the sense of failure that followed. Those invisible talent scouts had seduced me, and then let me down again; I doubted they'd come back. (And, indeed, they haven't.) One August morning—and it was this sudden—I awoke to realize that the weight of depression had lifted; I looked into the mirror, grinned at myself, and said, "Hi there. You're back."

And I'm still here, grateful for that chapter, but equally—no, more—grateful that it ended in apparent failure.

I still sometimes think about those folks who put up the sign but refused to vote. I tried once do to something bold, but it didn't work, and I haven't ventured into the larger arena again. In the end, I am content to be an advocate for others' activism—to put up signs, sign petitions, occasionally march, and hope for the best. I'm meant to be a small fish, swimming in a small pond, trying to live a principled life close to home. That's hard enough.

• • •

Sometimes, those signs come back to haunt me. Over the past two decades we've found many uses for the scores of red-and-white corrugated plastic signs with my name blazoned across the middle. White side facing out, they make great panelling on the cellar wall behind the washing machine and the freezer; doubled up, they provide a comfortable mat for kneeling tasks like weeding or painting baseboards; propped against an easel, they're a wonderful canvas for grandchildren's artwork. Even now, one is flat on the basement floor under the kitty-litter tray, easier to sweep over than the porous concrete. But eventually, we wanted to empty the shed. So, we carefully bagged most of them up—double-bagged, be damned the waste—and tossed them over the ledge at the municipal dump.

On a windy Saturday some weeks later, the phone rang. I answered to the raucous chuckle of an NDP friend. "Red and white Liberal signs with your name on them are blowing all around the dump."

A moment of horrified silence morphed into an hysterical laugh. "Fitting, somehow," I said, gasping for breath.

XVI   THE BOY FROM BELARUS

"They are going to give you their samovar!"

It's my daughter-in-law Katharina speaking. She has just rushed from the kitchen to the living room of an apartment in the Belarussian village of Chaussy, where I am already struggling with feelings of discomfort around the culturally fraught issues of generosity and appreciation.

There is no time to collect my thoughts. Inga and Alexei are standing in front of me; he is holding the ornate family samovar in his arms.

This story began on an early July morning two and a half years earlier, when Jack and I first greeted a sleepy ten-year-old with an elfin face framed by dark hair and punctuated by protruding ears. He emerged with half a dozen other children from a van that had carried them 700 kilometers from the Toronto airport to the small northern Ontario city of Sault Ste. Marie. The children stumbled off the van into a circle of families who had gathered to greet them. Their group leader was the last one off, carrying a single page which assigned one child to each family.

"And your boy speaks a little English," she said as she introduced us to the skinniest child of the group. "Viktor was with another Canadian family two years ago, but it didn't work out."

Two years before he had been eight, the age at which most of these children first left the security of their families to fly halfway around the world and spend the summer with strangers. Several of the children arriving on that early morning were returning for a second or third year; they knew their Canadian families and were welcomed with enthusiastic hugs. But Viktor hung back. I took a good look at him: a handsome child in shorts and a tee shirt, all ribs, knees, and elbows. He moved to stand with me and Jack, but it felt too soon for hugs.

These children were all from Chaussy, a small town in southern Belarus, which had the dubious distinction of finding itself directly under the cloud of radiation moving north from Ukraine after the 1986 meltdown of the Chernobyl reactor. They were part of a program, Children of Chernobyl, run by the Canadian Relief Fund for Chernobyl Victims in Belarus, an organization that brought children from the affected area to participating countries for the summer, giving their immune systems a rest from the constant barrage of radiation. Communities all over Canada and in much of Europe offered summer homes to these young Belarusians, providing them with fresh air, fresh food, medical and dental care.

When Viktor arrived at our house on that early July morning in 1996, his first act was to unzip his tote bag and proudly present us with gifts from his family: traditional Russian nesting dolls, delicately crocheted doilies, a photo book about Belarus, and a bag of hard candies.

He was slow to use what little English he had. For the first few days, his only word was "wow!" The house itself: wow! His own bedroom: wow! The dishwasher: wow! Our golden retriever: wow! Two cars? Wow! I squirmed as I began to see our affluence through his eyes. One day, when I opened the door to an attic-like storage area above our kitchen, he peered into the dusty space, cluttered with accumulated, no-longer used possessions, and uttered a new word: Why? At that moment, I was grateful for the language barrier. It was a question I couldn't answer.

He was a shy, solitary boy, rejecting most opportunities to join in with our friends' children or even his peers from Chaussy. Was this why his first summer in Canada had gone badly? Or was he just too young? Whatever the reason, he fit well into our recently-emptied nest. He rode his bike, ate mountains of fresh fruit, avoided vegetables, built exotic structures from Legos, played with the dog, and watched as much television as we would allow. He learned to drive the riding lawnmower—after asking why we had such a big lawn. We enrolled him in a two-week YMCA camp where he learned to swim and to paddle a kayak. We took him for medical and dental examinations—offered gratis by our family doctor and dentist. Although painfully skinny, he was deemed healthy. He endured a couple of small fillings without complaint.

Using his growing English vocabulary and stick figure drawings, he told us that he had an older sister, Anna, who was spending her summer with a family in Germany, that his mother worked in an office, and that the family had a "dacha"—a cabin in the country where they had a small vegetable garden. It was never clear what his father did.

By the time he left at the end of the summer, we had fallen in love with this little boy. We sent him home with vitamin pills for the whole family, garden seeds, gifts for his sister, and miscellaneous small kitchen gadgets that he coveted for his mother, as well as aluminum foil and zip lock bags.

The second year, he brought us an ornamental doll made from flax threads, a bottle of vodka, and several crocheted antimacassars which he told us his grandmother had made especially for us. He also brought a letter from his mother—translated by one of the organization's Canadian representatives—asking for an eye examination. Viktor was having trouble reading in school. And, she wondered, could we send her moisturizing creams and cosmetics?

By the end of that second summer, Viktor's English was close to fluent and we were beginning to see signs of a bright, inquisitive mind. He offered opinions about Russian aggression in

Chechnya (not good), talked about the Mir space station's name, (Peace), and told us about the gigantic mushrooms growing on the radioactive forest floor near his home. We sent him home with a pair of glasses perched on his nose, vitamins, garden seeds, more foil, plastic wrap, used plastic grocery bags, and moisturizers, lipstick, and nail polish.

Not long after he left that year, we learned that our son, Galen, and his wife, Katharina, were planning to spend a year studying in Moscow, and I began to hatch a plan. I wanted to meet Viktor's family and see this little village that sent its young away to live with strangers every summer, a painful migration forced by love and circumstance. I arranged to spend two weeks with Galen and Katharina in late October, with a side-trip for the three of us to Belarus.

•••

On October 31, 1998, at five am, we arrived after a sleepless night on the train from Moscow to Mogilov, Belarus, where Viktor's mother, Inga, met us along with a neighbour who had a car—a car that struggled to make the forty-minute drive through the still-dark Belarussian countryside to the family's apartment building on the edge of Chaussy.

Despite evidence of recent construction and the smell of new plaster, the boxy building managed to seem run down. But the apartment itself was nicely finished and well furnished. I was shown directly to the master bedroom which was to be mine for two days. Inga and Anna, Viktor's mother and sister, would sleep in the living room; Galen and Katharina were given Viktor and Anna's room; Viktor and his dad, Alexei, would sleep in the family's "other apartment"—which I gathered was where they used to live and was somehow still theirs. It's also where their phone was, which explained the difficulty we'd been having contacting them from Moscow.

Inga went straight to the kitchen and began preparing a feast. I followed her, offered help, but she shushed me out of the kitchen. No amount of protest was about to alter my status as guest of honour, so I sat with Galen in the living room waiting for Viktor to get up. Katharina was allowed to help, so she was chatting with Inga in the kitchen. She, whose cultural awareness was far greater than mine, assured me that I should feel honoured by all this activity on my behalf. It was, in effect, a gift. The first in a series of ill-conceived gifts.

I had been eager to see Viktor in his own home, to see his smile beam at seeing me. I had, as usual, imagined it all. But when he finally got up, he was sullen and quiet. Of course. My imagination hadn't taken into account that he was twelve years old and showing his Canadian "mom" a life I knew he considered inferior. No zip lock bags. No aluminum foil. He turned on the television which, throughout our visit, played an endless series of old American westerns with Russian voices dubbed over the still slightly audible English.

Inga served the feast around 9:30—salads, cold cuts, bread, cake, and champagne. Both Galen and Katharina could function in Russian, and conversation drifted around me on the wisps of Alexei's cigarette smoke. Although guest of honour, I felt barely present. After the meal, I slipped back to the bedroom and brought out the gifts I'd brought for the family. I gave Alexei and Inga theirs, but something was wrong. I didn't know what. They were not large gifts—more cosmetics, a small jack knife, a book about Canada—not unlike the gifts they sent to us, or that we sent back for them. But the air had become thick with excessive gratitude, bordering on rebuke.

As I began to hand Viktor his package, Inga spoke, and Katharina translated. "Later. You should sleep now." I had been ordered out of the kitchen, banished to the living room where

Viktor was ignoring me in favour of the television, my gifts were obviously somehow inappropriate, and now I was being ordered to bed. Nothing was going according to my plan.

I got up at noon to find the table set for yet another meal—this time chicken with all the salads and breads from earlier. And another bottle of champagne.

As soon as we finished eating, Galen and Viktor prepared to go with Alexei to get our return tickets to Moscow. I began putting on my shoes to walk along, but was not allowed. Too far. Katharina assured me again that I was being shown respect—for the role I'd played for Viktor and, um, and as an elder. Really? I was a bit over fifty. Probably ten years older than Inga.

The men left the four of us — Inga, Katharina, Anna (who had arrived home from her German school in Mogilov) and I —sitting in the living room with cups of tea. And now the mood shifted. We had three languages to work with, and Katharina spoke all of them. As she juggled Russian, German, and English, we all relaxed, laughed together, and the visit I'd imagined began to take shape.

I wanted to talk about the Chernobyl disaster, which had occurred when Anna was a small child and a few months before Viktor was born. Katharina, who grew up in Germany, talked about being kept inside for days as the radioactive cloud drifted over Europe.

Anna's response to that story spoke volumes. "In Germany, you weren't allowed to play outside, and here they didn't even tell us."

Inga talked about the fear and helplessness when they finally learned what they had been exposed to, about her fear for her unborn child—Viktor. She obviously had little hesitation about blaming the Soviet government of the time.

And how did it feel, I asked, to send so many of the town's children away every summer?

Of course, it's very hard, Inga said. But worth it if it helps them stay healthy. She is glad Viktor is happy with us because his first placement was not good.

"He was too young," she said.

I tried to imagine putting an eight-year-old in a van, en route to an airport in a city I had never visited, to fly halfway around the world to a country I couldn't imagine, to live two months with a family whose names and living arrangements were completely unknown. Yes. Too young.

The conversation moved to my plans, and Inga asked if I would be going to St. Petersburg. When I explained that there wasn't time for both Chaussy and St. Petersburg, she laughed out loud—and for the next two days, she shared this with everybody we saw—that I had chosen Chaussy over St. Petersburg.

When the men returned, I brought out my gifts for Anna and Viktor and immediately the camaraderie of minutes before evaporated. Why had I brought such expensive gifts, asked Alexei. But they were not. Some nail polish, fancy socks and a tee shirt for Anna. A watch—not an expensive one—for Viktor which was, as I insisted Katharina explain more than once, also a birthday gift.

As Inga, Galen, Katharina, and I prepared to explore the town, the tangled cultural expectations of giving, receiving, and gratitude weighed on my mind.

Over the next day and a half, I time-travelled to a century ago. It was not unlike my image of small Pennsylvania towns in the late nineteenth or early twentieth centuries where my grandparents were raised. Chaussy was certainly shabby, but I didn't find it depressing. The houses were small, frequently in bad repair, most with garden plots completely surrounding them. (I tried not to think about the radiation, the giant mushrooms in the forest.) But they were brightly painted, many with window boxes containing newly frost-bitten geraniums—it was early November. Most had outhouses and wood piles.

There were a few paved streets, a few cars, some tractors, bicycles, some horses and wagons, a motorcycle with a sidecar.

A tractor passed us, displaying a Canadian flag. Almost every family in this town had sent their children to Canada. Whenever we encountered someone on our walks, Inga introduced us as "Viktor's family", and then explained my choice of Chaussy over St. Petersburg.

The downtown was a mix of traditional and Soviet-style architecture. Inga, who worked as an accountant for the city, took us to her workplace. Here, the twentieth century had crept in. Several workstations were set up with computers—but no internet. The young office workers were so eager for its arrival that they insisted on taking our email addresses, promising to write.

The grocery store's mostly-bare shelves contained some meat, milk and cheese, a few bags of dry staples, lots of bread; the department store offered a small selection of housewares, clothes, and souvenirs. It was clear I was expected to shop, so I bought a bread board with an inlaid straw design that still hangs on my pantry wall. The small outdoor farmers market featured late fall produce—just a few squash, onions, turnips.

When we return to the house on the second day, another meal was being prepared — surprisingly by Alexei. Once again, I was banished to the living room.

And that's where I was when the samovar appeared.

"Because of all you've done for Viktor. We want you to have it."

"It's too much. So kind. But really, I can't." Katharina translated.

I knew I was walking a narrow line between ingratitude and insensitivity. Was this because I had brought gifts? But of course, there was no way I was taking their samovar. I was sure they didn't really expect me to. No, not true. I was not sure of anything having to do with gifts.

They persisted, but I sensed weakly, and in the end, when I explained that I couldn't possibly get it on the plane, they offered a bottle of vodka for Jack instead—which I happily accepted.

The samovar was on my mind the following July when the van pulled into the Sault Ste. Marie parking lot with the children from Chaussy. This would be Viktor's third and final summer with us. I watched anxiously as he retrieved his bags from the back of the van, assessing their capacity for carrying a samovar, and sighed with relief as I judged them too small. He brought us six crystal glasses and more crochet work from his grandmother. For which I expressed appropriate gratitude. Or so I hoped.

•••

All this was more than twenty years ago, and looking back I have no regrets about my personal experience. I came to love a little boy from another world, and I got a tiny glimpse of that world myself. I came away enriched. But it wasn't supposed to be about me, and I have to wonder whether we gave these children the gift we intended to give.

If the medical theory did, in fact, prove true—and I don't think anyone knows—then most people would judge the program worthwhile. But even then, in addition to strengthened immune systems, did we also send them home with unrealistic expectations and a predisposition to overvalue our privileged North American lives? Zip lock bags and aluminum foil were the tip of the ice berg. How can a ten-year-old understand the geopolitical, economic factors that allow him to ride in a new car in Canada, while in his entire home town there are no new cars, and the prospects of owning one are nil? How does he make sense of a table laden with fresh fruits and vegetables in Canada when the market shelves at home are bare? What are the social and emotional costs of emptying homes and entire towns of their children for several months a year? After several summers—and many children participated in the program well into adolescence—did the children find themselves lost between two cultures at the very time when they were trying to figure out who they are?

I've wondered for years. I don't have answers. I'd like to believe that every opportunity to experience another culture leads to both a saner world and greater self-understanding. I hope we didn't use Viktor as a way of burnishing our credentials as doers of good.

I wonder if these were some of the questions the government of Belarus was asking when the program to Canada was cancelled. It seems a number of Canadian host families made informal arrangements for their Belarussian children to stay indefinitely and attend school in Canada, which was never the program's intent. No surprise that the Belarusian government objected, and asked for a formal agreement with the Canadian government to prevent this from happening. Unfortunately, it insisted on including in that agreement a commitment that children would not be placed with gay couples. The agreement was never struck, and the last children from Belarus came to Canada in 2008.

We still hear from Viktor every few years. He is now a man in his thirties, living in Minsk, with a PhD in physics. He has worked in nuclear research and, as I write this, is a computer programmer for a US company whose founder was originally from Belarus.

In an email three years ago, he decided to come clean about something that had obviously been on his mind these many years.

"You remember that swimming pool that was broken and I told you that it was the big dog, Peso, did it? So, I broke it and I'm sorry for that."

I laughed until I cried. I don't remember the swimming pool incident at all, but I recognize the serious little boy who told a fib—

and grew up to be a man who felt obliged to set the record straight.

A few months ago, as I was writing this essay, I wrote to him again and reminded him of my visit to Chaussy. His reply warmed my heart and went a long way toward reassuring me.

"I remember too when you came to Chaussy and all those summers that I spent in Canada. They're very warm memories. You gave me a lot and pushed the boundaries of my mind and showed me another world which was drastically different from what I saw in Belarus in those days. It really encouraged me to develop myself."

Thank you Viktor. Better—far better—than a samovar.

XVII IT'S SUNDAY. IT'S MEXICO.

Extroverts sparkle, introverts glow.
Extroverts are fireworks, introverts are a fire in the hearth.
Sophia Dembling

Twenty-some years ago I sat in a university lecture hall listening to a presentation that changed the way I look at myself and other people. I don't remember the name of the presenter. Somebody-or-Other, Ph.D., whose talk was part academic lecture, part road show. He was good. I don't know if his evidence was, though a quick Internet search all these years later suggests the theory he presented is still in vogue. It's one of those "there are two types of people in the world" theories, of which we should all be suspect. Here's how it goes.

There is a level of cerebral stimulation at which humans function best, but at rest, people experience various levels of brain activity—which, I must say at the outset, is not correlated with intelligence. Those whose levels are naturally low feel a biological pressure to increase them, and so they seek out external sources of stimulation like social interactions, adventure, learning opportunities. These people—extroverts—are energized by such interactions.

Not so introverts, so the theory goes, whose brain activity at rest is naturally high. Their biological imperative is to ramp down. Introverts may appear to be outgoing, chatty, socially engaged. They may, indeed, enjoy the company of others. But they find social interactions and stimulation draining, and they must regularly seek solitude in order to recharge.

Most of us, of course, are somewhere along the continuum. Carl Jung himself, who first put forward this theory, acknowledged that no one could be on either extreme and remain sane. Still, I walked out of that lecture with my personal evaluation check-list and a new understanding of myself and my spouse.

"It's obviously because my brain, at rest, is just more active than yours." I wasn't bragging, just reporting.

"Which is why you're so happy doing nothing," he replied. He, too, had just taken the quiz and came out—of course—very high on the extrovert scale.

"I'm not doing nothing. I'm enjoying what's going on in my head. You wouldn't believe…"

"And I'm not really an extrovert," he insisted, turning up the car radio. But everybody knows he is.

He's the one who will turn "Hi, how are you?" into a fifteen-minute diversion in the cereal aisle while shoppers maneuver their carts around him and glare, reaching past him for the Raisin Bran. He's the one who can carry on a conversation in the car while listening to Leonard Cohen. He's the one who suggests we invite virtual strangers to dinner.

What I consider serene, he considers boring. What he considers stimulating, I consider chaotic. And what I considered a normal, comfortable, approach to retirement he called "sitting around and waiting to die."

Well, actually, I had more than that in mind.

Extroverts, who, according to some estimates, make up approximately two-thirds of humankind, leap into new endeavours with a fervour that leaves the less outgoing of us choking on the dust of their enthusiasm. They learn new languages and adapt to new situations quickly. They're energized by crowds and fireworks and wedding receptions—which is why they can't understand those of us who feel the need to retreat to the bathroom an hour after the party starts. They think we have weak bladders.

• • •

It is February, 1994, in the town of Patzcuaro, in the Mexican state of Michoacan. Midnight. The adobe walls of our small rental house are reverberating with the incessant bass rhythms of a band playing a kilometer away. Jack is sleeping through it. It's cool here in the mountains. I wrap a shawl around my shoulders and walk out onto the porch, where I look down on the town sprawling out below me and the lake to my right. Many houses are lit; a steady line of cars passes by on the secondary highway at the foot of the hill. The music throbs. No one is screaming *cállate!* Shut up! Why not?

February, 1998. This time, the city is Guanajuato in the Mexican state of the same name. Tonight it's music. Last night it was a soccer game. The television from the taco stand outside the bedroom window doesn't usually start blaring until the wandering minstrels have finished their tuneful parade through the narrow streets and performed a musical stand-up routine on the plaza just below us. We couldn't believe it when this quiet corner in which we'd rented a house for the winter turned into a nighttime fast-food and concert centre.

True to form, I bury my head under the pillow to blunt the noise. I have more trouble blunting the irritation. People live here. They try to sleep here. How can this go on? Until three a.m. Every night. We move to a different bedroom for the rest of the winter. A room without a window.

Also true to form, over the next couple of months Jack gets to know the taco stand folks.

We return three years later. And again, three years after that. Then, on the cusp of retirement, we buy a house in Guanajuato. We will not just sit around and wait to die. We will become snowbirds.

So little snowbird take me with you when you go,
to that land of gentle breezes where the peaceful waters flow...

February 2020. We are having dinner with Antonio and Eloisa, our Mexican family. The family with the taco stand has adopted us into their midst. Eloisa has made *pastel de carne*, which is basically meatloaf. It's delicious; she goes easy on the *jalepeños* when we're here. It's not possible to pass through the door into this home without being fed. And I don't mean tea and a cookie. No matter the time of day, there will suddenly appear quesadillas and soup, bowls of fruit and yogurt, or a full meal of rice with chicken mole and salad.

"Just like her mother," says Antonio. "She has to feed you."

I've given up protesting. I just eat.

I can't imagine the Mexican part of our life without these two, their children and now their grandchildren. They help us navigate parts of the culture that still seem strange to us. They include us in birthdays, holidays, even religious celebrations which they know we don't share. They entertain our grandchildren and bring us soup when we're sick. They were at our side that difficult winter here when Jack was ill and diagnosed with cancer. They have visited us in Canada twice.

Would this have happened if I'd stayed under the pillow, nurturing my irritation? Would I have learned to make tortillas in a Mexican kitchen? Would I have been *"mi abuela canadiense"* to two little girls?

We return to our own Guanajuato home, where a party is raging in the house across the small *callejón*, or alleyway—almost near enough to reach out and touch. The music is loud, the men drinking beer on the sidewalk are loud, occasionally a car pulls up playing its own loud music. The neighbourhood dogs join the chorus. No one is screaming *"cállate!"* I know no one will. I reach for my pillow.

The next morning, post-party, the woman on the roof across the *callejon* has her radio tuned to a local music station as she hangs out her wash. I've spent fifteen winters here, and I'm still not sure of the neighbourhood music etiquette—or even if there is one. As far as I can tell, whoever first plays music loud enough to engage (or enrage) the whole neighbourhood gets to choose the play list for as long as they like. Although late morning radio music from the rooftop might not be my choice, it doesn't enrage. But surely I can't be the only one who cringes when it's the hard-rock guy down the road who takes control of the neighbourhood vibe. Or when parties blare into the morning hours.

There are laws. If someone did complain, the police would come. This would not—in my staid North American opinion—be inappropriate. But am I about to do it? No. I own a house here. I pay my puny tax bill. I have attained formal resident status from the Mexican government. But it is not my country. Unless I felt someone were at risk—and I never have—I would no more call the cops on my neighbours here than call them to hush the crickets chirping in the fields beside my rural Canadian home. The sound is part of the landscape.

•••

"Why were they setting off firecrackers this morning," asks my visiting grandson.

"It's Sunday," I say. "It's Mexico."

It was also a Sunday my first morning in this country, January, 1994, the winter we spent in Patzcuaro. We arrived on the very day the Zapatistas began their rebellion and awoke to gunfire. We huddled, terrified, in our hotel room. Eventually we emerged to find other hotel guests having breakfast and lounging by the pool, apparently unperturbed.

"But, are we under attack?" I asked.

They looked at me strangely, then laughed.

"Oh, that! It's Sunday. It's Mexico." Then, something about alerting the angels to the souls of babies at the gates to heaven. But surely, not so many babies die every week. Surely.

We were nowhere near the Zapatista rebellion.

•••

Soon after that first winter in Mexico, I realized that I needed to learn Spanish. It shouldn't be that hard, I told myself. A lifetime ago, I studied Latin for four years, French for five or six. I haven't really used them, but I've lived in a bilingual country for most of my life. Cereal boxes and all that. I've been an editor. I'm passionate about language.

I registered for a university course, then a second one. Aced them. I could spot a subjunctive a mile away. Nuances of multiple past tenses? No problem. Ah, how I love grammar. A natural linguist!

Then another winter in Mexico. More courses, mostly conversation. Suddenly, my tongue and my brain were engaged in a stand-off. Here it comes, here it comes...the third person preterite is...gone. And while I grasped for it, conversation has moved on without me.

I watched Jack. He studied Spanish when he was younger, so it stood to reason he was more comfortable. But it was more than that. He talked. To everyone. All the time. Sometimes he made glaring mistakes.

"You said '*es bien.*' Should've been '*esta*'."

He laughs. "Right. You didn't say anything."

Well, yeah.

But then, I don't strike up chats with taxi drivers and street vendors in English, either. If someone asks how I am, I say "Fine, thanks." I can do that in several languages. It seems sufficient. It never occurs to me that the questioner wants to know about my recent recovery from the flu or the fact that I have opera tickets in my pocket. When the cab driver asks where I'm going, I tell him. I figure he can see the traffic congestion or the pouring rain better than I can, so why discuss it? When someone I've just met asks where I'm from, I say "Canada." Sometimes I add, "Ontario, near Lake Superior." I rarely launch into a description of snow depth and what minus forty feels like. I don't talk about how happy I am to be here. Maybe I should. My Spanish would be better. I'd probably seem friendlier.

Fifteen years and many classes later, I've given up. I no longer study. I speak haltingly, nervously, and forget vocabulary as fast as I learn it. I decided a few years ago to go with osmosis, which in fact allows me to absorb and comprehend quite a lot. But when I open my mouth, I usually wish I hadn't.

I only relax and let myself say foolish things and make hysterical mistakes with Antonio and Eloisa. They laugh with me and remember when I explained that we'd installed *aspiradoras* in the ceilings of the house. Vacuum cleaners? Really? I meant fans. *Ventiladoras.*

I wonder, sometimes, what happened to that confident linguist. The extrovert, by the way, is fluent.

• • •

It's *Dia de las Flores*—a pre-Easter celebration specific to Guanajuato. The streets are filled with couples who have been up all night dancing. They carry armloads of flowers amid the vendors that fill the narrow downtown plaza. The usually serene spot has been transformed into a warren of stalls and tables selling toys, hats, dolls, and plastic flowers of all shapes, colours, and sizes. As is always the case, the duplication of goods makes me wonder how anyone ever sells anything.

But what most impresses me today is the density of people and the toe-stubbing pace of movement through the plaza. My shoulders twitch from my inability to achieve even a modicum of personal space. Someone's recently purchased puppet stabs me in the left breast as I veer away from the mother with child in tow passing me on the right. There is no escaping the crush of bodies, and yet I must. I signal to Jack "I'm outta here" and wriggle rudely through the crowd until I reach the steps of the basilica, where there are actually a few open spots. I catch my breath and sit. I am almost trembling with relief. Jack waves from the swarm of bodies below, and I understand that he will remain in the crowd, which he finds stimulating. Later, we will walk home together and agree to disagree about the event. I will never again attend. He will go annually from now on and return with colourful photos that say "Mexico" to him.

• • •

The extrovert seeks to ramp up stimulation. The introvert seeks to dampen it. And so, my song to Mexico is a quieter one. The occasional early morning walk before the heat of day, when the streets are still and the only sounds are brooms making their endless journeys across the streets and sidewalks. The welcome I receive each winter from the butcher at my neighbourhood *carneceria* and the amusement in the eyes of the green-grocer at my local *fruteria* when

I carefully select two (just two!) *jalepeño chilies*. The smile on a child's face when I respond to a proud "good morning" in English with "Good morning to you." The sudden realization that I have understood a conversation at the next table, so perhaps osmosis is working. The thousand greetings to and from passersby. *"Buenas tardes...buenas noches...Adios..."* The growing familiarity with the city itself and its rhythms, feeling less like a tourist and more like one who belongs, albeit temporarily.

Night is falling quickly, as it does here. Two twelve-year-old girls are perched on the low wall outside our house sharing secrets. Beyond them, their brothers or cousins have divided into teams, shouting as they try to prevent the soccer ball from succumbing to gravity and bouncing down the steep hill. They are visiting their *abuela* on the other side of the *callejón*. She has no outdoor space, so the dusty, undeveloped area adjacent to our house is the playground of choice. They are making good use of it. The ball bangs against the metal *portón*. Someone shrieks. A toddler, too small for the game, runs into the melee and is rescued by a bigger cousin, who hands him—sobbing in protest—to the twelve-year-olds. He wants to be a big boy.

Someone kicks the ball too hard, and it flies over the wall and into our yard. More shouts, then "bang, bang" on the door to our patio. I set my book aside and open the door, knowing what I will hear. *"El balón, señora?"*

I fetch the ball, toss it back with a smile. The twelve-year-olds have joined the game, and the *abuela* is now sitting on the wall with the toddler and two babies, talking with her daughters who have come to fetch their children at the end of the day. Their husbands lean against the opposite wall, smoking and drinking beer. I exchange a few words about the evening, about the joy of grandchildren.

The game continues well after dark, shouts echoing off adobe walls, the ball banging into the *portón*, occasionally prompting a plea to find it on our side. Bursts of firecrackers send up small clouds of smoke over the city. An impatient cab driver honks his horn. One of the neighbourhood dogs begins a chorus and the others join in. Somewhere nearby, a marching band is playing.

It's Sunday. It's Mexico.

XVIII A NUMBERS GAME

I used to play a game with my age. The goal was to have at least half my life ahead of me, assuming I would live to eighty. Of course, in my twenties and thirties, it was a mathematical certainty that I would win. At forty-five, though, I would have had to live to ninety, which is a long shot. So I had to change the rules. The new goal was to have at least half of my sentient life ahead of me, which allowed me to discount my early childhood. Since I figured I wasn't fully sentient until about ten, I'd only have to make it to seventy. After fifty the game became even trickier; I started working with my adult life, beginning at twenty. By sixty, even with those rules, I couldn't win. Since I've never liked losing, I stopped playing.

• • •

It is 1998, and I am standing impatiently at the counter in the appliance department of Sears, the go-to place in my town for large appliances. I'm here because yesterday a loud, grinding noise from the basement announced that my clothes dryer of some twenty-five years had dried its last load. After examining dryers on offer, I am ready to place my order. But apparently the person on the other end of the telephone takes priority. I sigh audibly, and the saleslady gives me a nod, raises a perfectly arched eyebrow, purses her glossy lips, and holds up two fingers featuring pointy red nails. Two minutes. She looks like she should be selling cosmetics, not refrigerators.

The dryer will be delivered to the store in three days. I can pick it up there or wait another three days for delivery in my area. I will wait. And no, thank you, I'll pass on the extended warranty.

Finally, "Are you eligible for the senior's discount?"

I can't have heard that right.

"I'm sorry. Can you say that again?"

"Our ten percent senior's discount is available to anyone over fifty," she says.

In the silence that follows, I wonder if I could have dodged this question if I'd worn lipstick. I am over fifty, but I'm nowhere near ready to be a senior.

I want to say no. But ten percent of a dryer is a significant bit of cash.

"Well, I guess I am. Just barely."

But...how did she know?

On my way out, I wander through the women's clothing department, smiling youthfully at myself in mirrors while browsing through the end-of-season winter jacket sale. When I get home, I peer closely into the bathroom mirror. No wrinkles. A few grey hairs. A wee bit of chin sag; I will work on keeping my neck extended. Maybe I will consider streaking my hair. Just for fun.

I didn't feel like a senior. In fact, on the cusp of the new millennium, my life had suddenly taken the shape I had imagined for years. My freelance writing and editing business had expanded to include a half-time job as editor of an educational journal, work I could do entirely from home now that email and the Internet were widely available. Simultaneously, I had been asked to teach several sections of a freshman writing course at Lake Superior State University, just across the international bridge in Sault Ste. Marie, Michigan. I might be a late bloomer, but at last, when the time came to retire, I would have something to retire from.

The senior's discount question didn't come up again for some years. Only Sears had the effrontery to call a fifty-year-old "senior". Maybe that's why they went bankrupt.

• • •

It's hard to say anything new or meaningful about growing old. It's not for sissies. You're only as old as you feel. Age is just a number. I've earned every wrinkle. But sissies age too; there is no standard way to feel at any age; and you're going to get wrinkles whether you've earned them or not. You probably won't love them.

About the same time as I bought that dryer, I got my first bifocals.

"How are you finding them," asked the optometrist at my next appointment.

"They're not perfect," I said.

He nodded. "No. They'll never be perfect again."

Some years later, after cataract surgery, they almost were. But to compensate for the youthfulness of my vision, I was treated to a shocking view of my own face in the mirror, unfiltered by aging lenses. *Through a glass darkly, but then face to face...*

Glasses, hearing aids, knee replacements. All good. Never perfect. Ever again. And yet—true to the memes—I don't like to think of myself as too old for anything.

• • •

A couple of years ago, I decided I'd like to learn to play the violin. I needed something to challenge my sometimes-sluggish brain. I had considered returning to the piano—playing it more often—say once a week instead of once a year.

Or, given our post-retirement, part-time residence in Mexico, I considered hunkering down and finally mastering Spanish, another one of my half-baked enthusiasms that stalled somewhere near the "barely adequate" point along with gardening, quilting, and home renovation.

But for some reason, I found myself thinking about the violin.

My mom played the violin in her high school orchestra. I only know this because there was a violin in our attic when I was growing up. I never heard her play it. My youngest son, given the choice between piano lessons and violin lessons at the age of eight, chose the violin. At first, we were told he had real potential.

"A good ear," they said at the conservatory.

Maybe so, but his dedication was minimal. That chapter in his life ended after a few years when I left his violin in the trunk of the car on a hot May day. When he arrived at his lesson, the instrument tumbled from the case in several pieces. His teacher was not amused, and my own chuckle stuck in my throat when I remembered that the violin didn't belong to us. We had it repaired, returned it to the conservatory, and he abandoned music lessons, leaving behind the lingering strains of Twinkle Twinkle Little Star in its multiple variations along with images of cats racing for the door.

When I casually mentioned my late-life interest to a friend who teaches strings, she lent me her back-up violin and a beginner's book. (Is there a student, anywhere, who doesn't begin with Twinkle Twinkle—a tune composed by Mozart, as it turns out?)

Within a few weeks, I wanted a violin of my own.

My community has many virtues, but a supply of stringed instruments for sale isn't one of them. When I mentioned this via Facebook to a good friend who lives in Ohio, he said, "I have a violin. I haven't touched it in forty-five years. I'd be pleased if you had it." And so it transpired. The instrument arrived in perfect condition after its long rest, and turns out to be a very fine violin, made by a well-known luthier in Germany in the 1950s.

Too good, really, for nursery songs. This was getting serious.

Google Search 1: Learning violin as an adult.
Result: It's like a combination of kindergarten and physiotherapy.

The kindergarten part was pretty obvious. It's the physicality that most amazed me. Hold the bow with your fingers just so: thumb bent at the frog, middle finger holding the stick in opposition to the thumb, first and third fingers curled gently around, little finger balanced on the top. And it has to stay that way. Then there's the neck-and-chin maneuver in which the violin sits effortlessly against the shoulder, cupped by the chin, requiring the left hand to hold no weight, thereby freeing its fingers to flit nimbly from one string to the next while the bow glides across them at a right angle, somewhere between the bridge and the neck. Oh, and did I mention how important it is to stay relaxed?

I am reminded of those childhood vacation days on the New Jersey shore, when we entered the surf right in front of our parents' towels and umbrella and, within moments, had drifted a great distance down the beach only to be hauled back and told to stay within sight. And once again, without any sense of it happening, we drifted.

So it is with my bow. I try to keep it perpendicular between the bridge and the neck. But somehow, nearly two years after I began this adventure, it still drifts off at a weird angle. Unlike my mother, whose voice showed patient concern as we continually floated away, the violin screeches at me. "What the hell are you doing? Don't you know I'm better than this? I was made for Beethoven!"

Google search 2: Learning the violin as a senior.
Result 1: "As a senior citizen, you should make it a point to do all the things you always wanted to do in your life...Today, learning to play the violin can be as simple as purchasing a series of online video tapes."

Moving on, then...
Result 2: "It's hard to get around the stark reality of math when you pick up the violin as an [older] adult," says Liz Bayne in the Ottawa Citizen.

Here's that reality. If you practiced for half an hour every day, it would take fifty-five years to meet Malcolm Gladwell's 10,000 hour rule, the theoretical time it takes to achieve mastery of almost anything. An hour a day would still extend well beyond my life expectancy. What about settling for just adequate at, say, 2,000 hours? That would only take eleven years.

Did I mention I am seventy-five? Obviously, I am not meant to win at number games.

•••

Time has passed just as my mother said it would, as her mother and grandmother told her it would. Faster and faster, until finding those lost years is like trying to identify a hummingbird from a speeding car. After what seems like forever, you're finally twenty; ten years later you're thirty; forty rushes to meet you in less than a decade; fifty pounces on you unawares; when you wake up the next morning you're sixty, and by lunchtime, you're sixty-five. Eighty will be here before I figure out what my next sentence should say. No one knows how this happens, but it happens to everybody.

Equally mysterious is how the perception of time becomes tangled in the web of memories. We re-roofed the house fifteen years ago. I'm sure, because that's the year we went to England and I bought those green gum shoes there, and I remember wearing those shoes going up the ladder to give Jack the roofing nails. It's the same year we got the orange cat, so she's sixteen. But was Y2K really before that?

The older I get, the more memories hover on peripheries of my mind, ready to leap to the forefront at the slightest suggestion. But there's something else. Not exactly a memory, but a sensation I refer to as being "struck young"—the feeling that every possibility is still open, that the world stretches out endlessly into the future. I can't conjure these moments up at will as I can memories— say, learning to ride a bike in my childhood driveway or the furniture in my freshman dorm room. They visit unannounced, and for a fleeting moment I am seventeen and on my way to college. Or thirty with a baby at my breast. Or twenty-two on a spring morning. All that is to come has not yet come. This is as close to time travel as I can imagine, and the sensation evaporates as quickly as it materializes, leaving me gazing at a horizon that grows ever closer.

All this reminds me that we're supposed to understand time as a relative concept, that somewhere out in the universe it doesn't even exist. This is beyond my comprehension. My son, Galen, tried to explain it to me once years ago using an analogy of two trains passing. I think he lifted it from his first-year physics book. I didn't get it then and I don't get it now. But it reminds me of a lecture by Richard Dawkins in which he explained that our brains have evolved to function in the "middle world". We struggle to comprehend both the molecular and the cosmic because understanding them doesn't help us navigate our reality. At the molecular level, we may know that the wooden table consists largely of empty space, but we can't quite process that information because it doesn't relate to our experience. If we based our behaviour on our understanding of physics, we would be covered in bruises.

So it is with time. I am here in the middle world, and time is out there in the cosmos. There's no question that it appears to speed up as we age, but whether or not a year is always a year, or becomes less of a year when two trains rush past each other, we all arrive at Christmas on the same day, so —however relative it may seem—there must be something fixed about it.

•••

It is four o'clock in the morning and I am lying awake. This is the fretful hour, when gremlins creep out of the recesses of my brain to remind me that the planet teeters on the cusp of ecological disaster; that madness in high places is changing the world, probably forever; that I won't be part of that forever long enough to see how my children and grandchildren fare in an uncertain future. The gremlins are in fine form tonight, stoking the fires of anxiety, seeding fear in the fertile soil of darkness. Perversely, time moves in slow motion now—a minute. Five. Twenty. I pound the pillow, shift onto my back and stare at the shadows on the ceiling.

A warm breeze through the open window sets the venetian blind trembling, and I get up to raise it above the opening. The summer sky is already beginning to lighten. I pause at the window to watch the stars, their light crossing the millennia, then fading into the pale emptiness of pre-dawn.

Out there, somewhere, time is laughing at me.

An abridged version of this essay appeared in the Fall 2010 issue of La Presa.

XIX SEASONAL DISORDER

The earth does renew itself; we don't. And so we want to connect our human cycle of mere growth and decay, where winter holds no spring, to the natural cycle of renewal. We can't do it, of course, but we can't stop trying
Adam Gopnik, "Winter: Five Windows on the Season,"
CBC Massey Lectures, 2011

Something in the air has turned to fall. Oddly, not the temperature, which continues in August mode, mid to high 20s. Evenings are a bit cooler than they were a month ago, but I'm still kicking my covers off in the middle of the night. Environment Canada says it will be 33 degrees Celsius in Toronto today—definitely August. Definitely a changing climate. The leaves aren't really turning, though there are a few hints on the hill. Still, something has changed. The light, perhaps, or the sound of the crickets chirping all day. Maybe it's the heavy morning dew. Whatever it is, it's unmistakable.

I'm glad. Fall is my favourite season. I'm still waiting for the crisper mornings and the sparkle of frost on the grass, but I know they will come.

The anticipation of seasonal change is bred in the bone. I've given that a lot of thought since we started avoiding the season that defines Canada. Not so much the changes themselves; I'm in Canada to experience three of the four seasons, and it might be argued that I've romanticized the fourth over the nearly two decades that I've avoided the worst (or best) of it. But I wonder how this cycle of annual decay and renewal, and its metaphorical significance, affects the way we see ourselves and the world.

I mentioned this once to a Mexican friend, suggesting that perhaps the cycle of seasons, with their dramatic differences, has created a different sense of self and time in those of us who live in less temperate climates.

She leapt into defensive mode: "We have seasons too you know."

Of course. I hadn't meant to offend. I said different, not better. If seasonal change has a metaphorical significance for me, then no doubt it does for her as well. But the drama of annual death and rebirth isn't her metaphor. She doesn't experience the miraculous appearance of tiny leaves pushing through frozen ground, the frantic rush to grow from seed to flower and back to seed in a few short months, the shortening days and the long nights of winter. Hers must be a gentler rhythm than mine, though it too involves births and deaths, small miracles of nature. Dry brown hillsides turn green with the coming of summer rains; chilly breezes seep under unsealed doors, announcing a winter cold front; deciduous trees drop and re-form leaves according to a timetable of their own.

Mexicans are famously comfortable with death. Its inevitability sits easily beside their enthusiasm for life, while we northerners rail against it. Along with Dylan Thomas, we rage against the dying of the light. Are we each reflecting our formative experience with seasonal change?

•••

Even though I know I will be gone for the winter, I have piled a small stack of firewood outside the back door, easily accessible for feeding the old-fashioned wood cookstove in my kitchen where, on colder days, I like to simmer soup or fry bacon. I hang damp gloves or freshly washed shirts on a rack nearby to toast dry beside the fire. I light this fire only a few times a year now. What used to be a life style has become nostalgic ritual.

There are so many things I like about winter in the north: wood fires in that kitchen stove; snow swirling against the windows in blizzard-winds; the tightening of cheeks and chin against the cold; the quality of light and shadow created by a sun, low on the horizon, reflecting on a white world. And perhaps best of all, the sense of suspended animation—a stretch of months when a blanket of snow conceals all of summer's unkept promises, a time of connection and contemplation, a season of short days asking little and long evenings asking less.

I'm not a Pollyanna. I haven't forgotten the frozen water pipes, the endless shovelling, the cars refusing to start, the painful cold of wet feet and wind-propelled snow pellets, the winter days that invade the April calendar. But poking through the discomfort, always, a proud sense of entitlement: When spring came, I had earned it.

"What?" says Jack. "You need to earn spring?"

He speaks as the primary breadwinner who scraped the windshield and shovelled the end of the driveway before driving half an hour every day on winter roads. As the primary fix-it guy in the partnership, who thawed frozen pipes and fussed with reluctant motors. And as a man who—it seems incontestable—has a biological thermostat with a set-point quite different from my own; he suffers dreadfully from the cold. While I am opening my jacket and pulling off my mittens on a sunny winter afternoon, he is shivering under his many layers. And when I take his hand in mine, it is ice against my warm palm.

It has now been more than a decade since I've earned spring. Again this year, trying to understand, Jack says "Let's stay home for a few weeks in January so you can have your fix of winter. I just don't want to put up with months of it." But he misses the point. Of course, winters in northern Ontario can be long, brutal, and dark. But it's the "putting up with months of it" that entitles you to the prize.

He insists—only somewhat in jest—that I have a mental disorder. How can anyone enjoy being cold and miserable? I point out that I am no fan of discomfort. It is not about the temperature or the snow—although there is little more beautiful than a fresh snowfall. It is about a personal cycle of hibernation and resurgence—reflection followed by a call to action—a cycle that mirrors nature's own progression through the seasons in northern climes and which, for me, defines the passage of time.

When bears hibernate, they emerge in the spring cranky and hungry. It's different for me. I rarely deprive myself of nourishment in any season. Indeed, I think of winter as a time to nourish both body and soul. Unlike the bears, I emerge a bit plumper and energized, ready to tackle the tasks and pleasures of the next three seasons.

This is what I was trying to communicate to my Mexican friend. And this is the cycle that Mexico—for all its pleasures—has broken for me. Just as the time comes to comfortably turn inward—when the garden is harvested, the leaves raked, the deck furniture stored away, when the dark comes early, and I have pulled the afghans out of the closet and piled the winter-reading, as heavy as the afghans, beside the sofa—at that moment, I find myself flying over the encroaching winter and landing in a place where it never gets dark before seven and where flowers bloom all winter.

It has always amused me that in Mexico the first day of spring prompts celebrations and parades, small children dressed as bright flowers, confetti on the streets. This fine-tuned awareness of a change that is barely perceptible to my northern sensibilities occurs annually, a few weeks before I return home to find the first signs of rhubarb, garlic and crocuses poking through the last of the winter's snow.

By then, the back of winter is broken. April nights continue to drop below freezing, but the days have lengthened, the sun is higher in the sky, and the mid-day air is soft on the face. The first robin appears, often ahead of the first worm. I throw open the living room windows just for the freshness of it, and enjoy the fact that warm days arrive ahead of black flies and mosquitoes. We can look forward to a month without bugs.

And yet…there are no parades. Children slough off their tired snow suits in favor of windbreakers, hoodies, and mud-suits—but they don't dress as daffodils. Why, I wonder, do those of us who experience some of the most dramatic seasonal changes on earth allow them to pass without public celebration?

During these first days at home, I capture the tail end of the quiet season, when the earth is coming back to life but asking nothing of me. For a few weeks, I pretend to awaken slowly from a sleep I haven't actually taken. I re-settle, reconnect with friends, watch the wet ground gradually absorb the huge puddle in the back yard, and listen to the melt water rush through the ditches from the hill to the river. The bears have already emerged and are prowling the bush, hungry. By mid-May spring has arrived with a vengeance and, like the shrubs and flowers, I feel an irresistible urge to move on with the season. Once the deck furniture is out of the shed and the hill is turning the magical green of early spring, I am beginning the annual tasks of re-claiming the perennial bed, poking vegetable seeds into the damp, warm soil, and driving the mower around the absurdly large lawn.

Despite endless promises that, this year, summer will be quieter, a more relaxed and reflective time, it is never so. Children and grandchildren visit; outdoor projects demand attention while weather permits; a family wedding calls us out of town for a week; I have tickets to the Stratford Festival again this year. By late August, when the hills begin to dull and the vegetable garden is heavy with produce, I will be spent.

I will eagerly await the coming of Fall, when I will once again prepare for the season of quiet reflection. I will stack wood and pull winter clothes from the back of the closet. I will light several fires and wear my extra-heavy coat once. Then I will board a plane and fly to my other home, where I will sip wine beneath the eucalyptus tree and yearn for blizzards and frigid air and snug fires. And wonder if I really do have a mental disorder.

• • •

It is mid-March, and I am sitting under that eucalyptus tree, looking at the shadows of cactus and bougainvillea on the adobe wall, watching the swallows swoop under an archway to their nest in the corner of the portico. The evening air is cool, a relief after the heat of the afternoon which creeps upon us as the time for our departure looms. Yes, there are seasons, and it is spring here, though it feels like mid-summer to me. I am thinking of my imminent return to the cool, moist air of northern Ontario as it slowly inches into a very different spring. The air is filled with butterflies that have emerged from their own quiet times in the cocoon, and I wonder if the bears at home have emerged from their hibernation. If I had been there, I would be beginning to stir, to breathe in the exhilaration of spring after the months of cold and dark.

Now, of course—fickle person that I am—I am reluctant to leave. Like a child struggling with the concept of permanence, I long to defy the laws of physics, to be in two places at once. And yet. Something deep within in me needs to be rooted.

The time is rapidly approaching when I will need to choose where I want to spend my final years. I know that my two-story brick farmhouse, the house I made my home, half an hour's drive from basic services, may not be suitable for an octogenarian. Many Americans and Canadians have chosen this Mexican city. It's an attractive milieu for retired folks. A comfortable climate and an endlessly stimulating cultural life. The local population is welcoming, and I've made many good friends here among the ex-pats. It's a caring community. It would wrap me in its arms. Sometimes, it's tempting.

But no. When the time comes to end this double life, I know I will choose a place where the seasons speak my language. Where I can hibernate, look through frosty windows at the raging elements, perhaps, if I am able, venture into the icy fray to test my mettle, and return again, all the more grateful for the warmth and comfort of my nest. Where I can reflect and recharge, in anticipation of however many springs remain.

Sections of this essay were aired on CBC radio's The Sunday Edition *in 2013.*

XX FLOWING ON

Water, water, see the water flow...Oh wizard of changes, teach me the lesson of flowing.
The Water Song, Incredible String Band

It's a lesson I'm still struggling with. Although I have recently become an enthusiastic apologist for denial of the inevitable, reality leaps into my consciousness from time to time and leaves me by turns frightened and determined. Alone and afraid, alone and courageous. Alone. For more than half a century, I've been a partner, a wife. Over the decades our lives have become so entwined that it is difficult to know how we would disentangle them. But we're old. Did I actually think we were immortal?

I'm thinking about this—and the insecurity that has taken over our lives since Jack's cancer diagnosis a few years ago—as I sprawl on a rocky expanse overlooking Lake Superior. Uncertainty has never been easy for me, and when confronted with it I try to prepare by engaging my imagination, by role-playing possible outcomes—mostly bad—in various scenarios. I've always done this, whether the outcome to be feared is as trivial as an abscessed tooth or as dire as an early death. Jack calls it catastrophizing. I call it preparing for the worst.

Whatever it's called, I'm engaging in it here, my body firmly supported by some of the oldest rock formations on earth, listening to the water lap against them, and staring up at a blue, blue sky.

I am hiking along the lake with friends today. They have left me perched on this rock while they walk a little farther. Would I come here alone? Would I keep our little cabin by the lake? Could I figure out the plumbing by myself? Would I re-arrange the furniture? (And what does it say about me that I have a plan for that?) Would I still laugh and tease and share bad puns, or would I lapse into a sad and bitter old age? Would I...Will I? Jack is doing well now, but I can't seem to stop my imagination from spiralling downward.

And then. With the heat of the rocks warming my back, and a breeze off the water rustling the sparse grasses that poke out from mossy clumps, a feeling of sheer contentment overtakes the catastrophizing, reminding me that this lake can still calm my soul.

I don't remember my first glimpse of it. It may have been when friends visited us shortly after we moved to the farm. They arrived with kayaks atop their car—a common sight now, but a rarity then. They had heard about the sand beach at Batchewana Bay, an hour's drive north. We spent a pleasant afternoon there, but I don't recall experiencing the sense of wonder that I've come to associate with Lake Superior.

Sometime later—the precise chronology is unimportant—I travelled a bit farther north with friends to spend a day on another beach, this one featuring the smooth, multi-coloured stones that are common on the lake's many bays, and with dramatic rock outcroppings defining the periphery of this small cove. It was a beautiful spot, but I was preoccupied with watching my toddlers and visiting with my friends.

It wasn't until we began spending days, and then weeks, camping as a family along the shore, that I began to feel Mishibeshu, Ojibway spirit of the lake, creep into the marrow of my bones.

"This is where God lives, if there is a god," I said, still open to that possibility.

Those were the years of running a family farm, holding down jobs, concerns about children's behaviour or academic success, and—for me—constantly second-guessing the life I led and the choices I'd made. No different, I suppose, from the lives of most.

At the campground, we were just one family among many with tents or pop-up trailers pitched in spacious campsites. This was not wilderness camping. Children rode bicycles on the mile-long road that followed the pebble beach, couples walked their dogs, families scurried up the boulders and headlands that marked the edge of the campground, and teenaged dare-devils leapt into the frigid water from the rock cliffs. On some evenings, we walked to the visitors' centre to see films or nature presentations, then returned to sit around the campfire roasting marshmallows. It was the stuff of a million North American summer holidays.

Except for the magic. And here I stumble, because I don't know how to put the magic into words.

Photos hang on the walls of my memory. A perpetually angry child softens and sits in stillness on the rocks. An adolescent, leans against a log, wrapped in a blanket, staring into the vastness. A small child throws pebbles into the water, watching the expanding ripples.

Sometimes it comes quietly. A mist drifting across the water, an improbable pine growing from a crack in the rocks, the lull of waves lapping against the beach, the expansive view of water interrupted by majestic headlands, one after another, fading into the distance, an ancient, petrified echo. And sometimes it comes in with a roar as storms gather over the water and turn the lake into an angry inland sea. The fury of Mishibeshu. However it arrives, it carries with it the power to transform my chronic catastrophizing into acceptance of whatever the moment holds. It sucks out tension and replaces it with a calm wonder.

It was that small pine tree that spoke most loudly to me. Summer after summer, I left the campsite behind and scrambled up the headland at the end of the campground. A dozen long steps up, over jutting rocks, around the rock face and along a narrow, moss-lined path worn bare by decades of campers, to a huge, smooth rock surface where I perched, knees pulled close to my chest, gazing at the blue expanse, sometimes smooth as glass, sometimes sparkling with small ripples, sometimes crashing in breaking waves, throwing up spray. I was more often than not alone, although occasionally I interrupted an embracing couple or was interrupted by a gaggle of ten-year-olds. Invariably, as I stared down at the lake, I sang under my breath: Oh wizard of changes, teach me the lesson of flowing.

I didn't have a song for the tree, but if the water was a wizard of changes, the tree was a wizard of steady, sturdy resilience—a white pine, bent away from the water by the prevailing wind, stunted by the meagre nourishment its roots could garner from the small rock crevice. Not much bigger than a seedling, but with old gnarled branches and coarse bark. How long, I wondered, had it been here? On my annual visits, over two decades, it seemed unchanged. I haven't visited that spot for many years now, since we abandoned the campground for a little cabin on the lakeshore. I wonder if my tree is still there, if I'd recognize it, if others also marvel at its resilience.

Of course, resilience is everywhere, as is magic. Stunted trees struggle out of rocky crevices all along the lake—pines, spruces, birches. There is magic wherever the timeless pulls us away from the fears and anxieties that fill our quotidian lives. For me, it is here, on this rock and rocks like it, my body pressed against a surface smoothed by millennia of glaciers and moving water, listening to the lake trying—still trying—to teach me the lesson of flowing.

Afterward

It is the middle of March, 2020. I am at my weekly writers' group meeting at the Embajadoras restaurant in Guanajuato, where the five of us have just finished discussing whether the coronavirus is something we should be seriously worried about. Some of us wonder if we should change our plans to travel home—to Canada or to the U.S. Would it make sense to leave sooner than planned? We agree on a general "wait and see" attitude and bump elbows with a laugh. It's probably another false alarm. Remember the swine flu?

Lee is just beginning to read her poem when my cell phone rings. I ignore it. It rings again. It is rude to deal with a cell phone when someone is reading a poem, so I ignore it again. By the time the waiter brings me the restaurant phone with an urgent voice on the other end, Jack is already in the ambulance. He's had a seizure at lunch with friends. The cancer, which was discovered in his kidneys four years earlier, has moved to his brain.

We arrive at our daughter's house in Kitchener, Ontario, a week later, just a few days after the Prime Minister has requested all Canadians to return. Borders all over the world are slamming shut in what turns out to be a futile attempt to control the virus. Our lives are slamming shut, too. Our personal medical crisis has converged almost precisely with the global one. Even the two-day stay with our daughter before driving home is in violation of the 14-day self-isolation rule for residents returning from out of the country.

• • •

Jack's driver's license is suspended because of the seizure. It is jarring to see him always in the passenger seat. At some point it dawns on me that I will never sit there again.

He sells his beloved sports car.

He transfers all the automatic payments to my credit card and insists on reviewing with me financial matters I've largely ignored, passwords I've never known, how to change the water filters.

"I'll figure it out," I say.

"Let me help you prepare," he says. "It's the most important thing I can do."

I weep, learn to change the filters.

We make several trips a week to the hospital for appointments and treatments, wearing masks. Because he is a palliative cancer patient, I am allowed to accompany him most of the time, despite covid restrictions. Except for these medical appointments and a couple of trips to our cabin on Lake Superior, he never leaves home.

At some point in the summer, he develops an aversion to any dry food and I begin making meals that feature gravy. Eventually, he tolerates only soup—which our daughter-in-law provides almost daily.

He works in his pottery studio in the mornings, naps in the afternoons, reads in the evenings. We begin watching more TV than we ever have. He gradually weakens, has trouble concentrating, begins to lose his balance, walks with a cane.

He maintains an attitude of acceptance. "I've had a good run," he says. "I've been a lucky man." He says this especially when he speaks of our children, who gather around him more and more often as summer turns to fall.

Throughout, we are grateful for the care—and the caring—he receives from friends and professionals, much of it remote as covid controls the details of the world beyond the circle of home.

When a severe seizure sends him to the hospital by ambulance in September, we know the end is near. He returns home, which is where he wants to be, but the man I know, the man I have lived with for 54 years—through the proverbial, but so very true, good times and bad—that man is gone. Together, we experience the ebbing away of his life until a day comes when the life continues, but I am the only one of us experiencing it. A few days later, it is over.

•••

As I write this, I have been living alone for more than a year, in semi-isolation thanks to the pandemic. I have spent a lot of time sorting through and thinking about the stuff of my life—the things that I've accumulated, the decisions I've made, the friendships that have sustained me, those I've left behind, the choices that lie ahead. I have tried to maintain an even keel.

Though time continues its headlong dash, I am not in a rush to move on. I will stay in this place I love until it feels right to leave. Everyone says I will simply "know", so I await that revelation. Perhaps it will never come. I will sell the house in Mexico, because I *do* simply "know", though I have not ruled out spending time in Guanajuato, the city that has become a second home.

And I will try to live in the present. That's a struggle sometimes. *Now* is only one breath long, and often hard to capture. With so much more of life behind than ahead, the past elbows in whenever it's given the slightest encouragement, and memories can be as comforting as those old quilts tucked away in the upstairs closet. As triggers of thoughtful reflection, memories are among our most precious possessions. But if we're not careful, they can suck the oxygen out of the present and discourage imaginings that fuel the future.

In this collection of essays, I have tried to use the past as a route to discover some perspective and coherence in the unfolding of an ordinary life—and hopefully to elicit in readers some recognition of shared experience.

Gradually, I am emptying the upstairs closets of material things that no longer speak to me; the quilts may go soon. I am adjusting to the shape of my new reality and allowing myself to lapse into occasional reveries of nostalgia. But I am also trying to listen for and hold on to what this moment, this day have to offer—the intangible stuff of a life that, for now, continues to move forward.

Paula Dunning is a writer of memoir, essays, and short fiction. She lives on a sprawling property of fields and forest along the Echo River, near Sault Ste. Marie, Ontario. Her memoir, *Shifting Currents,* was published by Embajadoras Press in 2016, and she regularly blogs about matters large and small, as she sees and experiences them, on her website at www.echoriver.ca

What readers say about *Shifting Currents:*

Beautifully written, by turns wry and poignant, *Shifting Currents* turns a landscape into a heartscape you will never forget.
        Bill Roorbach, author of *Temple Stream, Life Among Giants,*
        The Remedy for Love and *The Girl of the Lake.*

A memoir that reads like a novel, with prose so clean it sparkles.
        Lilly Barnes, poet and author of *Mara* and
        The Adventures of Goygla.

You have made me laugh and cry. A good combination in the stress of today's world.
        Annie Smith, poet

If you've ever entertained for one minute the fantasy of making your own maple syrup and milking your own cow, I'm sure you'll enjoy this wry and loving look at living the rural life.
        Elizabeth Creith, author of *Shepherd in Residence*
        and *Erik the Viking Sheep*

Shifting Currents is available on amazon.com and amazon.ca and on the author's website at www.echoriver.ca